"SECOND HAND HIGH, THIRD HAND NOT SO HIGH"

NO RULES, JUST RIGHT

JAMES MARSH STERNBERG MD (DR J)
AND
DANNY KLEINMAN

authorHOUSE·

AuthorHouse™
1663 Liberty Drive
Bloomington, IN 47403
www.authorhouse.com
Phone: 833-262-8899

Published by AuthorHouse 07/12/2021

ISBN: 978-1-6655-1989-2 (sc)
ISBN: 978-1-6655-1988-5 (e)

Library of Congress Control Number: 2021905324

Print information available on the last page.

This book is printed on acid-free paper.

CONTENTS

PART I: SECOND HAND HIGH

PART II: THIRD HAND HIGH, LOW, OR OTHER NOT TOO HIGH

DEDICATION

For ALAN and STEVIE, my first partners.

Thanks for so many good memories. It was a great ride.

---JMS

For ROSE and HYMIE

without whom this book would never have been written

---DK

ACKNOWLEDGEMENTS

This book would not have been possible without the help of several friends. Frank Stewart, Michael Lawrence, Anne Lund, Randy Baron, and Eddie Kantar all provided suggestions for material for the book.

We are forever indebted to bridge Hall-of-Famer Fred Hamilton, the late Bernie Chazen, Alan Brody, Norman Gore, Dick Recht, and Norbert Jay without whose guidance and teaching we could not have achieved whatever success we have had in bridge.

And, of course, Jim wants to thank Vickie Lee Bader, whose love and patience helped guide him thru the many hours of this endeavor.

James Marsh Sternberg, MD   Danny Kleinman, Psephologist
Palm Beach Gardens FL   Los Angeles, CA

INTRODUCTION

"Second hand low" and "third hand high" are so-called rules we learned in Bridge 101 along with others like "cover an honor with an honor" and "always return your partner's suit." These so-called rules will get you by, but they won't bring you very far.

Second hand must become familiar with certain basic exceptions to foil declarer's plans, often by playing second hand high. Likewise, many contracts are decided by the play of third hand, usually at trick one. While at first playing high may seem obvious, a little thought may help you find a killing defense.

Being a slave to either "second hand low" or "third hand high" will lead you down Desolation Row. Take time to review what you know from the bidding and play. Does this deal call for passive or active defense? We hope that the examples in this book will awaken you to a wider variety of options for defenders.

Sometimes the right play is unclear. You may have to make decisions before you have enough information. But that's part of the fascination of bridge. If everything were automatic, the game would lose most of its appeal.

The hands are arranged in chapters by theme, but there is some overlap. We're sure you will recognize situations from your own experiences at the table. We hope this book will spur you to think more and take nursery rhymes with a large grain of salt.

While all four hands are displayed, we urge you to look at only your own hand and the dummy. Try covering the other two hands temporarily, revealing the unseen cards only after choosing your plays. With practice, you will make the good plays that a player in the first room misses, but his counterpart in the second room finds.

They play at IMPs, at an *Open Room* and a *Closed Room*. Overtricks matter little, so defenders seek only to beat contracts.

PRELUDE

This book discusses defense, the most difficult part of bridge even for experts. Yet in half the deals you play, especially if you are a sensible bidder who likes plus scores, you will be defending.

If you are bored by bad cards, you will be a loser, guaranteed. Instead of thinking about the game, you will spend your time lusting for aces and kings, or perhaps the blonde at the next table. Wouldn't you rather beat contracts, or at matchpoints, which most of us usually play. stop overtricks?

That's the bad news, but it's also the good news. By paying attention, you'll succeed better than the rival who spends his time ogling the blonde when he holds those boring bad cards, but is required to finish out the deal.

In many of the deals you declare, your opponents will have been silent throughout the auction. In the deals you defend, they will have bid. If you find yourself asking, "Whose lead?" at the end of the auction, you've already blown it, for the defense starts with the first bid of the auction. Oops, did we say, "with the first bid"? We should have said with the first *call*, which likely as not is a pass.

If you deal and pass, you should be thinking how the missing HCP are divided among the unseen hands. Whether you bid or pass, *eavesdrop* on the conversation between your opponents. Try to anticipate which opponent will be declarer.

If you think it will be your left-hand opponent (LHO), consider lead-directing bids and doubles when your right-hand opponent (RHO) makes an artificial bid such as a transfer, Stayman, or New Minor Forcing. If you are on opening lead, guess the shapes and strengths of the other three hands before leading. When you see dummy, you can revise your guess.

If your partner is about to lead, guess which suit he'll lead. When he leads some other suit, you'll often be able to figure out why. That's just one of the reasons to take time to think before playing to Trick 1. Even if you know what you're going to play. Even if it's a singleton. You've just seen 14 new cards, and you have lots of new information to digest.

For example, you should be thinking what partner's holding may be in the suit he led and wondering why he led it. Perhaps because in some other suit he has the ace without the king. It's almost as though you'd used Blackwood.

You have some planning to do. If declarer leads an honor from dummy at Trick 2, will you cover? If declarer leads a singleton from dummy, will you rise with your ace?

In *"Why You Lose at Bridge"*, S.J. Simon advised us to think what to lead to the next trick before deciding whether to win this one. That applies more broadly than he may have imagined. Think whether to cover the next honor before ducking this one.

You're entitled---nay, expected---to take time at Trick 1. Nobody can draw any inferences therefrom, not declarer and (more importantly for those of us who love the sport of bridge) not your partner.

The subtitle of this book refers to "rules," but the only genuine rules of bridge are those to be found in rulebooks (the "Laws"). Other things that many misguidedly call "rules" are mere conventions and guidelines.

Let's discuss conventions first. Declarer's plays are all *cardplays*: attempts to win tricks that can be won and avoid losing tricks that needn't be lost. Defenders' plays are often simply cardplays. But they have a dual function: they are informatory, conveying information to partner that may help him defend. That makes them conventions.

You may be familiar with informatory plays as signals, showing attitude ("I like this suit, please lead it again!" or "Please lead some other suit!"), count ("I have an even number of cards in the suit"), or suit preference (a high card showing a liking for the higher of two other suits).

Think of signals as luxuries. You can't always afford them. Many contracts slip through defenders who have fallen in love with signals. A defender discards the ♡Q intending to say, "Partner, I like hearts!" only to discover later he *had* a heart trick until he threw it away.

The authors of this book fall in love only with girls. When it comes to a choice between the right cardplay and the appropriate signal, choose the cardplay. Those who fall in love with signals overlook the girl next door. *The right cardplay can be as helpful to partner as the most glamorous signal.*

Here's an example. Your left-hand opponent opens 1NT and plays there. Partner leads the ♣4 and you see ♣865 in dummy. You have ♣QJ9 and partner is probably leading from a holding like ♣K1074 or ♣K10742. After dislodging declarer's ♣A, the defenders will come to three or four club tricks. The one club you must not play is the ♣Q. That is the club you would lead if you were leading the suit.

If you play the ♣Q, declarer will win the ♣A. When partner regains the lead, he will not continue clubs but will wait for you to get in to lead a club (if you have one) through declarer's supposed remaining ♣Jx. He may wait forever 'neath the streets of Boston.

By contrast, suppose you play the ♣J. When declarer plays the ♣A---*if* he plays the ♣A---partner will know you have the ♣Q, else declarer would have won it at Trick 1. In this example, the right cardplay also conveys accurate information.

Why is the ♣J the right cardplay? Because it obeys the *right* rule. In following to a trick, a defender's job is to *use the lowest card that will do the job.* The job here is to win the trick or keep declarer from winning a cheap trick. The ♣9 would do the job if the ♣10 were in dummy, but the ♣9 won't do here, as partner *may have* led the ♣4 from ♣AK742. In that case, the ♣9 would let declarer win a cheap trick with his ♣103.

Note that the rule as stated is distinctly better than "Third hand high," but it too should sometimes be broken. Each of the "rules" discussed here should be taken as a *guideline* prefaced by the clause, "*In the absence of a compelling reason to do otherwise ...*" What might such a reason be? One possible reason might be a desperate need to get partner to shift to an obvious alternative upon regaining the lead.

Here's another: Partner's lead is the ♣4 again and you hold ♣QJ10 behind dummy's ♣86. You suspect that partner may have led from ♣A9742. If you play the ♣10, declarer with ♣K53 will win the ♣K. When partner gets in, he may think your ♣10 is from ♣J10x. Again, he will wait for you to get in and lead your ♣J through declarer's supposed remaining ♣Qx.

However, if you play the ♣J to Trick 1, you throw him a sandwich. Placing the ♣10 with declarer, and perhaps also the ♣Q, partner can continue safely with the ♣9 to declarer's presumed ♣Q10, risking nothing but a club trick that he could always establish for himself.

Won't partner be pleasantly surprised when you turn up with both missing club honors and he runs the suit! Of course, you needn't make such clever third-hand plays as ♣J from ♣QJ10 when you expect to obtain the lead before partner.

Other "rules" for defenders govern *which card to lead* in a suit *once you decide to lead it*. Yes, these are conventions. These are sometimes presented in a list with the most desirable holdings from which to lead at the top. However, that list must be taken with a very large hunk of salt: *"in the absence of other information."* In other words, only for "blind" opening leads, as after1NT-2NT-Pass.

Even then, the lists were drawn up before transfer bids and Stayman were invented, so that dummy was as likely to have length in a major suit as length in a minor. Those days are gone, and *all else being nearly equal*, you'll do well to prefer majors to minors in close cases.

As Mike Lawrence emphasizes in his fine book on Opening Leads, choosing the right suit to lead based on the auction is usually more important than choosing the suit with the most promising holding.

Once dummy appears, neither the opening leader nor his partner remains blind. That should suffice to rebut the maxim "Always return partner's lead," which ignores the vast difference between leads made before seeing dummy and leads made with dummy in plain sight.

"Fourth highest from length and strength" often enables partner to know when *not* to return a lead.

A typical example arises when West leads the ♡2, or any heart that East can identify as his lowest, against South's 1NT. East wins Trick 1 with a doubleton ♡A and sees two or three hearts in dummy. Placing declarer with four or five hearts, East knows *not* to return his remaining heart until his last chance to do so, when the defenders are ready to cash out.

"SECOND HAND LOW"? "THIRD HAND HIGH"? NOT SO FAST

At best, these two slogans are guidelines, not rules. Remember, you are not playing "Simon Says," you are playing *bridge*. Or rather, you are playing one of many forms of bridge. Let's digress to list and discuss them briefly.

(a) Rubber bridge.

(b) "Chicago" or some other variety of four-deal bridge.

(c) Total Points, a form of duplicate bridge for teams that resembles four-deal bridge.

In these forms of bridge, you are playing for *points* as defined by the scoring chart. It is relatively easy to calculate what is at stake, for those points show up on the scoresheet.

Suppose both sides are vulnerable without any partscores and you have bid 4♠. Ten tricks earn your side 120 points and a 500-point bonus, a total of 620 points. An eleventh trick adds a piddling 30 points, not worth worrying about. Down one costs your side 100 points, but that is just the *visible* cost.

The hidden cost is the 620 points you don't get. The *swing* is 720 points. That's much more to worry about than 30 points for an overtrick or 100 points for an additional undertrick.

(f) Matchpoints. Here nearly every point can be worth worrying about ... or not. If you wind up declaring 3◊ when your counterparts declare 1NT and make an overtrick (120 points), your overtrick becomes crucial.

Make that overtrick (130 points) and you earn a top. Make your contract on the button (110 points) and you earn a bottom. Sometimes, however, your counterparts can take only seven tricks in 1NT, and just making 3◊ suffices for a top.

Sometimes you should play as though it were rubber bridge (just make the contract), but sometimes you should try for every trick that is not tied down.

(g) Board-a-Match. This was the form of contest for teams in duplicate bridge tournaments until the mid-1960s. Think of it as matchpoints *but* instead of 25 grades of success (0 to 12 matchpoints, with halves possible), there are only 3 grades (win, lose or draw).

Some very fine players deride matchpoints as "not real bridge." They are mistaken. Matchpoints and perhaps to a greater degree Board-a-Match
require all the skills of other forms of bridge plus another. You must judge which to maximize: your *chances* of success (making or beating the contract) or your *degree* of success (how many *extra* tricks you take).

Filling the gap between (c) and (f):

(d) IMPs. A compromise between Total Points and Board-a-Match.

(e) IMP-Scored Pairs. A compromise between four-deal bridge and matchpoints. It has become commonplace in casual competition as played on the Internet.

These forms of bridge are much more like four-deal bridge than matchpoints.

In this book, you are playing a team match at IMPs. Your goal and the goal of your partners, opponents and teammates will be to make a contract when you declare, or break a contract when you defend.

We will show you first how the play went in the first room, the Open Room, where it is typically sloppy, and then how it went in the second room, the Closed Room, where the play is more skillful.

Let's get started.

RULES FOR DEFENDERS

Some bridge teachers instruct beginners as if they were teaching Latin grammar or long division. They teach "rules" and algorithms. "Always" and "Never"; Step 1, Step 2, Step 3; "Do this, don't do that, can't you read the sign?"

For example, this "rule" for a defender who is the third to play to a trick: "Third hand high!"

Then, instead of admitting candidly that their "rules" are wrong, they take great delight in finding "exceptions," much like the Ptolemaic astronomers who portrayed the Solar System as consisting of circular orbits with oodles of circular epicycles to account for the observed discrepancies. Rules and exceptions, like circles and epicycles.

"Rules are made to be broken"; the "exceptions" are dizzying and dazzling, which goes to show what a marvelously difficult game bridge is. You need to memorize the exceptions to get everything right.

"Always cover an honor with an honor!"? That's has as many epicycles---er, we mean *exceptions*---as "Third hand high!"

May we, like the astronomer Kepler, suggest an ellipse? The right rule: "Cover an honor with an honor only when by doing so *you have a reasonable chance of promoting a trick in the suit for your side.*"

Notice that the *right* rules include mention of the *purposes* behind them: to keep declarer from promoting intermediate cards as tricks and to promote intermediate cards as tricks for the defenders.

It takes little skill to win top tricks. The battleground for tricks in the play of the hand is for tricks with *intermediate* cards, the tricks the defenders can promote for themselves and keep declarer from scoring.

Example (1): Matchpoints, East-West vul

NORTH (dummy)
♠ J 4
♡ 8 7 6 3 2
♢ 8 3
♣ Q 10 7 5

EAST (you)
♠ Q 7
♡ A Q 10
♢ K J 9 4
♣ 9 6 4 2

South opens 2 NT (20-21 HCP) & declarer is in 3♥ after a transfer auction. Partner leads the ♢2. Plan the defense.

You have 12 of the partnership's 16 or 17 HCP, and will most likely obtain the lead before partner. Wouldn't you like to know the location of partner's 4 or 5 HCP? You know he doesn't have the ♢A, no underleading on this auction. But he might have the ♢Q. Play the ♢J. If it loses to the ♢A, your ♢K is a winner. If it loses to the ♢Q, you will know partner's strength lies elsewhere.

So you play the ♢J. Declarer wins the ♢A and leads the ♣3. Partner ruffs. What do you know? It is obvious declarer is trying to reach dummy to start trumps. So you know declarer has the ♡K. Since partner has the ♢Q and 2 or 3 HCP elsewhere, which can only be the ♠K.

What can you do now? You can follow with your lowest club, the ♣2, as a suit preference signal showing the ♢K. Partner will return a diamond so you can give him a second club ruff. After winning the ♢K, you will lead the ♣9, your highest club spot-card, as a suit-preference signal telling partner that it is safe for him to underlead his ♠K.

Besides two club ruffs, you and your partner will collect one diamond trick, one spade trick, and the ♡A, thus beating the contract. Must you work all this out to know to play the ♢J at Trick 1? No, if you use the *right* "rule" for third hand play, the "Prevent Defense": *Prevent declarer from taking tricks with cards you can keep him from scoring.* "Third hand high!" is simply the *wrong* rule, a circle when we need an ellipse.

Example (2) Matchpoints, North-South vul

NORTH (dummy)
♠ K 7 2
♡ 6 4
◊ J 5 3
♣ A J 10 6 2

EAST (you)
♠ J 8 6 5
♡ K Q J 7
◊ 6
♣ Q 7 5 4

SOUTH	WEST	NORTH	EAST
1◊	Pass	1NT	Dbl
2◊	2♠	3◊	All Pass

Partner leads the ♣9; declarer covers with dummy's ♣10. Plan the defense.

Partner's ♣9 can be top of two or a singleton. If the ♣9 is top of two, then you must also play low, in order to remain with a stopper after the first two rounds of clubs have been played. If the ♣9 is singleton, you must still play low, in order to block the suit.

Look what will happen when the ♣9 is singleton and you play low. Declarer will draw trumps to keep partner from ruffing clubs. Suppose declarer has ◊AKQxxx, the most favorable case for him. He can draw trumps ending in dummy and lead a low club, finessing the ♣8 successfully when you follow low.

Then declarer can cash the ♣K and try to reach dummy by leading his singleton spade. However, partner will be able to take the ♠A and shift to hearts. Declarer will win the ♡A, but have no way to reach dummy. He will take six diamonds, three clubs and one heart trick, ten tricks in all.

Declarer will do better to lead his singleton spade before playing a third round of clubs. Then he can use dummy's ♣A as an entry to the ♣K and take eleven tricks instead of ten. Look at what happened after East covered dummy's ♣10 with the ♣Q, however. Declarer drew trumps, cashed the ♣8, and wound up with twelve tricks: six diamond tricks, five club tricks, and one heart.

WHAT'S WRONG WITH THE "RULES" FOR DEFENDERS?

Most of us rely on shortcuts that we think of as "rules," of which "Third hand high!" is a prime example. If you needed to pick one simple rule to use, that might be it, but it suffers from three serious defects.

(1) Inaccuracy. We can remedy this defect by reformulating the "rule": *Third hand's job is to keep dummy and declarer from scoring preventable tricks in the suit led, and he must play the lowest card that will do this job.*

Even this rule is not entirely accurate. Here are some reasons it isn't.

(a) Sometimes we must sacrifice a trick in the suit led to protect two or more tricks in another suit.

(b) Sometimes we must play a different card to make it easier for partner to go right later in the defense.

(c) Sometimes we must play a different card to make it harder for declarer to go right later in the play.

(2) Perspective. One play may be best to maximize the number of tricks in the suit, while a different play may be best to maximize the chances of beating the contract.

(3) Technique versus Information. A defender must take into account not only the tricks at stake in the suit, but also the information conveyed by the card he plays, so that his partner will not go astray subsequently. Usually such information benefits his partner more than declarer. But sometimes a defender may know that declarer will be the main beneficiary and so he must withhold or distort information.

PART I
SECOND HAND
HIGH

PROTECTING
PARTNER'S
ENTRIES

SECOND HAND PLAY

When most of us were beginners, we were taught that when declarer led low from hand or dummy, the defender had one of two tasks: to follow low to the lead of a low card, or to cover an honor with a higher honor. That was it, the end of Bridge 101.

However, that is only the beginning of good defense. In the main, covering an honor may accomplish any of three things, and two out of three are not good.

Here's the one that is good: covering may *promote* a trick in the suit for you or your partner. Here are the two that are bad: covering may *compress* your tricks and your partner's, or may *eliminate declarer's guess*. When you face a "duck or cover?" problem, you must judge the effect of covering. Sometimes you can know for sure. At other times you can only make an educated guess, aided by the bidding, and putting yourself in declarer's shoes by asking yourself, "From what holdings might declarer lead the card he did?"

The truth is more complicated still. Let's examine some basic positions in which second hand has more to do. This often involves playing a higher card than Mother Goose recommends.

Before examining particulars, let's note the general conditions that require second hand to rise with a high card. Among the most common:

(a) Entry Preservation. Let partner keep his entry for use later, when the suit he is trying to develop for tricks has been established. The defender who is short in that suit must hop up with his stopper in dummy's or declarer's long suit so that his partner's stopper will be available as an entry later.

(b) Duck Prevention. Sometimes you are the "Danger Hand" that declarer may need to keep off lead for fear that you will lead through his (or dummy's) fragile stopper in your partner's suit. Then you must rise with your honor in declarer's or dummy's long suit to keep declarer from ducking a trick into the "safe" defender's (your partner's) hand.

(c) Preventing a *Ruffing Finesse*. Hearts are trump, but this is the club position:

Dummy
♣ Q J 10 9

Partner   You
♣ A 6 4 2   ♣ K 7 5 3

Declarer
♣ 8

If declarer leads the ♣Q from dummy, you'd better rise with King Louis lest he fall under the guillotine on the next club lead.

(d) The John Donne Coup. When the hand that will be third to play has inside entries to a long suit but no outside entry, second hand must often rise and shine to force declarer to burn the inside entry prematurely. For example, in a notrump contract, declarer leads the ♣2 in this layout:

Dummy
♣ A K 10 9 5

You   Partner
♣ Q 3   ♣ J 8 6 4

Declarer
♣ 7 2

The lady is for burning. The ♣Q is destined to die regardless, but by jumping into the flames now, she forces declarer to burn a scarce dummy entry to kill her now, preventing declarer from inserting dummy's ♣9.

If you cover declarer's ♣2 gently with your ♣3, will your partner let dummy's ♣9 win heroically?

But wait! Maybe the lady shall live after all. Declarer is Sir Galahad, and he won't let her die. *What would you play from* ♣QJ3, ♣Q63 *or* ♣QJ63 *if any of these were your holding?*

We trust you would play the ♣Q, or sometimes the ♣J. [In situations like this, they are hermaphrodites whose sex we can seldom distinguish.] Now declarer's best hope for four club tricks is to let the ♣Q live and guess next round whether to finesse dummy's ♣9 or play for a 3-3 split.

But since that I must die at last 'tis best
To use myself in jest,
Thus by feigned death to die.
---John Donne

SOME SUGGESTIONS FOR SECOND HAND PLAY

In these examples, declarer has no outside entry to dummy.

Figure 1

♣ Q 7 2

♣ A 9 5 4   ♣ J 10 8 3

♣ K 6

Eager to reach dummy to finesse in some other suit, South leads the ♣6, hoping to gain entry with the ♣Q. West thwarts this effort by rising ♣A.

Hard to read! If South actually has ♣K63, ♣K1063, or ♣KJ63, by playing the ♣A *on air*, West blows a trick, his own ♣9. So unless you're quite certain of the layout, listen to Mother Goose this time.

Even if South has flashed his clubs to you, you'd better be *sure* that dummy has no entry elsewhere. Might dummy's innocent-looking ◊9543 turn out to supply a fourth-round entry?

Figure 2

♣ A J 10 3

♣ Q 9 5   ♣ K 8 7

♣ 6 4 2

South hopes to score three club tricks by finessing twice. When he leads the ♣6, a routine "second hand low" ♣5 from West will let him succeed. By rising with the ♣Q, however, West holds South to two tricks, as it forces declarer to use dummy's sure entry, the ♣A, prematurely---*before* East's ♣K has been dislodged.

Note that swapping West's ♣9 for dummy's ♣10 makes little difference (declarer probably intends to "deep finesse" dummy's ♣9).

Would swapping West's ♣Q for East's ♣K change anything?

Yes! Feminists will be pleased to learn that a queen may be more potent than a king. When West's honor is the king, he is doomed. Declarer will almost surely finesse. However, when West's honor is the queen, she may be safe. For declarer may have ♣K8642 and play for a 2-2 split, or he may plan to finesse East for the missing ♣Q on the second round.

Might declarer have ♣87642? If so, rising with either member of the royal couple may lead to a menage-a-trois with dummy's ace, who swings both ways and will enjoy that greatly. So until you learn otherwise, Mother knows best ... even if she is a Goose.

When declarer leads an honor from dummy, a simple guideline usually suffices to steer you right. It's usually right to cover a lone honor led from dummy, but to wait for *your last opportunity to choose* when dummy has more than one card that may need covering.

Some teachers may tell you to "wait for the last of dummy's equal honors to cover," but that is not exactly right. They probably learned it from Mother Goose herself. If you hold ♣K9 behind dummy's ♣QJ2, cover that queen as soon as she is led, for if you play the ♣9 now, the card your ♣K will cover next turn may be the ♣2, not the ♣J. If you hold ♣K10 behind dummy's ♣QJ9, the reward for covering dummy's first honor will be greater still: a trick for your ♣10 when declarer finesses dummy's ♣9 next.

When declarer leads an honor from his hand, your "Duck or Cover?" dilemma is more severe still, as you cannot see his other cards in the suit.

As a helpful guideline, assume that if dummy has only one honor in the suit, declarer is likely to have two. With only one honor in his hand, he most likely would have led towards it from dummy. So you'll usually do best not to cover immediately if you can wait for the next chance to decide.

That is not without risk. Sometimes a weak declarer will take a "Chinese Finesse" (though we've not seen any of our Chinese-American friends try one): leading a queen towards dummy's ace-deuce when he doesn't have the jack. You'd better cover when that happens, but the Peking Duck is the tastiest item on the menu when declarer has QJ10.

Sometimes a strong declarer may prey on your gullibility by taking a Chinese Finesse as his only hope. Bob Hamman's worst nightmare is declaring against two Peter Fredins, one on his left and one on his right. Danny's worst nightmare is defending against Peter Fredin when Peter leads a queen through his king with dummy showing ace-low behind him.

Figure 3

♣ A 6 4 3

♣ K 7 5　　　　　　　　　　　　　　　♣ Q 9 2

♣ J 10 8

As dummy has only one honor, West must duck the first honor that declarer leads and wait for the second, no matter in what order declarer plays them. If instead West covers the first honor, declarer will have a finessing position through East. It matters not if we swap the ♣K and ♣Q. The king and queen sleep equally comfortably on either side of the bed.

Figure 4

♣ A J 8 6 5

♣ Q 7 2　　　　　　　　　　　　　　　♣ K 9 3

♣ 10 4

Now dummy has *two* honors, so West cannot presume that declarer has the missing ♣K when declarer leads the ♣10 through him. Should West cover?

Yes, if the layout is as diagrammed above.

No, if declarer has any of several other holdings, including ♣K10943, ♣K1094 and (embarrassingly!) ♣10943.

That's another reason for paying keen attention during the auction and taking some time to think before playing or turning your card to Trick 1.

Figure 5

♣ K 10 9 8

♣ Q 7 6 4　　　　　　　　　　　　　　　♣ A 5 2

♣ J 3

When declarer leads the ♣J, West must not cover because dummy's club spots are strong enough to gobble up West's three low clubs once the ♣Q is gone. *Cover only when you can hope thereby to promote a trick for your side.* Here ducking can earn West a fourth-round club trick after South establishes and cashes the two club tricks available to him.

Figure 6

$$\clubsuit \text{A J 4}$$

$$\clubsuit \text{K 8 5 3} \qquad\qquad\qquad \clubsuit \text{7 2}$$

$$\clubsuit \text{Q 10 9 6}$$

No matter which honor declarer leads, West must not surrender his ♣K, as it is his only club that is high enough to win a fourth-round trick after dummy's ♣A is gone. Of course if the honor that South leads is his only club honor, West will blow a trick by ducking.

See Figure 4: more tricks may be lost by ducking there, but West will nonetheless blow one trick by ducking here if declarer's holding is ♣Qx or ♣10x.

The bidding will sometimes tell you declarer's length or strength in a suit, but not always. If you can't stand the uncertainty, take up chess or checkers.

"DUCK OR COVER?" QUIZ

In each case, you are defending against a notrump contract, and after winning Trick 1 in some other suit, declarer puts you to the test in clubs.

For simplicity's sake, we shall assume that declarer dealt and his 1NT opening ended the auction, so you have no clues except from his notrump range and the play to Trick 1. Not much help for you today!

#1.

$\clubsuit$ Q J 3 2

$\clubsuit$ K 5 4

Declarer leads the $\clubsuit$Q from dummy: duck or cover?

#2.

$\clubsuit$ J 7 6 4 3

$\clubsuit$ K 8 2

Declarer leads the $\clubsuit$J from dummy: duck or cover?

#3.

$\clubsuit$ A Q 4

$\clubsuit$ K J 6

Declarer leads the $\clubsuit$9 from his hand: duck or cover?

#4.

$\clubsuit$ A 7 4 3

$\clubsuit$ Q 6 5

Declarer leads the $\clubsuit$10 from his hand: duck or cover?

#1.

♣ Q J 3 2

♣ K 5 4

Declarer leads the ♣Q from dummy. *Duck.* Wait to cover dummy's ♣J on the next round, the last time you'll have a choice. If you cover now and declarer has ♣A98, declarer can finesse against partner's ♣10, but by covering dummy's ♣J on the second round, you'll *promote* partner's ♣1076.

#2.

♣ J 7 6 4 3

♣ K 8 2

Declarer leads the ♣J from dummy: *Duck.* Although it is usually right to cover a lone honor, dummy's five-card length means you'll score your ♣K later if you can score him at all. Yes, if declarer has ♣AQ5, you'll blow a trick, but do you really think he'd start with dummy's ♣J if that were so?

More likely, however, declarer will have ♣A1095. A wily declarer may even have ♣Q1095 and drop his ♣Q under your ♣K if you cover. The ♣K won't enjoy the resulting menage-a-trois despite the presence of a fourth honor in this extreme example of *compression.*

#3.

♣ A Q 4

♣ K J 6

Declarer leads the ♣9 from his hand. *Cover* to *promote* a trick for partner's possible ♣8532 or stronger. If declarer finesses dummy's ♣Q and returns to his hand to lead clubs again, cover his ♣10 but duck his ♣7.

#4.

♣ A 7 4 3

♣ Q 6 5

Declarer leads the ♣10 from his hand. *Duck.* To cover declarer's ♣10 can't promote any club tricks for the defense, but may *compress* a trick if partner has a bare ♣J, or any doubleton that includes the ♣J. If partner has a bare ♣K, covering may cost two tricks, for with ♣J10982 declarer may have planned to finesse twice.

Even if partner has only low clubs, covering will spare declarer a *guess* that he might otherwise get wrong.

Second Hand High to Protect Partner's Entry

Suppose your partner leads the ♣Q against a notrump contract, and you are East:

```
                    ♣ A 5
♣ Q J 10 8 7                        ♣ 9 4 3
                    ♣ K 6 2
```

Declarer ducks and partner continues with the ♣8 (original fourth highest) to dummy's ♣A. Your side must get in twice; first to dislodge the ♣K, then to cash two winners.

Now you must do all you can to win the next defensive trick, hoping to preserve partner's entry until his suit has been established.

This is so important that normal guidelines do not apply. For example, if declarer leads dummy's ◊Q to Trick 3 ...

```
            ◊ Q J 9 4
                        ◊ K 7 6
```

... you would ordinarily duck, waiting to cover dummy's ◊J next. This time, however, it *may* be necessary to step up with your ◊K. You are risking the loss of a trick or two if partner has ◊10xx and carnage if he has a singleton ◊A to gain two tricks when partner has a *doubleton* ◊A.

If instead you duck, the price for heeding Mother Goose may be the two club tricks that partner can establish but no longer cash.

DEAL 1. SECOND HAND HIGH VERSUS NOTRUMP

```
                    ♠ Q 5 4 3
                    ♡ Q 10 4
                    ◇ J 9 6
                    ♣ 10 9 7
      ♠ 10 8 2                      ♠ K 9 7 6
      ♡ K J 9 7 6                   ♡ 8 2
      ◇ 5 2                         ◇ 10 7 4 3
      ♣ A 3 2                       ♣ K 5 4
                    ♠ A J
                    ♡ A 5 3
                    ◇ A K Q 8
                    ♣ Q J 8 6
```

Despite North's Stayman 3♣ response to South's 2NT, West led the ♡7. Declarer played dummy's ♡10 as East followed with the ♡8 to show count. Declarer started clubs with dummy's ♣10.

Desperate to retain his club entry, West let the ♣10 hold, but South abandoned clubs and ran home by finessing the ♠J next. Nine tricks.

How did the defenders beat 3NT in the other room?

South, Third Hand Hymie received the same opening lead and put up dummy's ♡Q. Then he led a sly ♣7 from dummy.

"Did you really mean to call for the *seven*?" asked Second Hand Rose, East. "Not through the Iron Duchess!"

"Duchess is my receptionist," answered Hymie, but Rose put up her ♣K like a man. She shot the ♡2 back in a flash and took care not to revoke for the rest of the deal. Her partner eventually took three hearts and another club for down one.

Rose's play would not have succeeded if Hymie had the ♣A, but in that case, she figured, no other play would succeed anyway.

DEAL 2. PROTECTING PARTNER'S ENTRY

```
                    ♠ A 4
                    ♡ K 5 2
                    ◊ Q J 8 5
                    ♣ 7 6 4 3
   ♠ Q J 10 8 2                  ♠ 7 6 3
   ♡ 8 7                         ♡ 10 9 6 4 3
   ◊ A 9 4                       ◊ K 7
   ♣ J 9 2                       ♣ Q 10 8
                    ♠ K 9 5
                    ♡ A Q J
                    ◊ 10 6 3 2
                    ♣ A K 5
```

West led the ♠Q against South's 3NT and continued with the ♠8 when it held. Declarer called for a low diamond from dummy and covered East's ◊7 with the ◊10. West, desperate to retain her diamond entry, ducked.

South wasn't about to give the defenders a second chance. He played clubs from the top, and when they split 3-3, he had nine tricks without a second diamond trick.

When they compared with their teammates, they saw that in the other room, Hymie went down in 3NT. "Why didn't you make it?" asked East.

"It's that silly Rose," said Hymie. "She grew up on the Lower East Side and visited a second-hand bookstore on Second Avenue. She bought every bridge book she could find. She remembered 'Second hand high, third hand low!'

"So when I craftily called for a low diamond at Trick 3, she hopped up with her king and cleared spades. If you'd read your Mother Goose, you'd have won it too." "No," said East. "It's second hand low, third hand high."

"I never remember which it is," said West. Rose may never have read Mother Goose, but she figured if South had the ◊A, he would have led dummy's ◊Q or ◊J to Trick 3. She realized the urgency of getting in to lead a third spade while her partner still had the ◊A for an entry.

Would she have ducked had Hymie started with a quack from dummy? We don't think so.

DEAL 3. SECOND HAND HIGH VERSUS A SUIT CONTRACT

```
                        ♠ K 9 6 3
                        ♡ Q 10 8
                        ◊ J 10 3
                        ♣ A K 5
        ♠ 5 4                          ♠ A 2
        ♡ J 4 2                        ♡ 7 6 5 3
        ◊ K 9 7                        ◊ A 8 5 4 2
        ♣ Q J 10 7 2    Moshe          ♣ 6 3
                        ♠ Q J 10 8 7
                        ♡ A K 9
                        ◊ Q 6
                        ♣ 9 8 4
```

Despite North's 1♣ opening, West led the ♣Q against South's 4♠. Moshe, who was still recovering from retinal surgery, won dummy's ♣K and called for the ◊J, letting it ride as East played the ◊2 in tempo.

When West won the ◊K, Moshe struck his forehead with his free hand and moaned, "Oh, I thought *I* had that card."

His mistake didn't hurt him. West persisted with the ♣10. After winning dummy's ♣A, he tried to slip the ◊3 past East.

Crying "Oh no you don't!" East rose with the ◊A and led a third diamond, hoping West could ruff, but it was South who was out of diamonds and discarded a club. It was all over but the shouting. Making 4♠.

Do you think the defense could do any better in the other room?

There, in the same contract, Hymie, South, won the club lead in dummy and called for a low diamond at Trick 2.

"Trying to steal a singleton honor, Sweetheart?" asked East, Rose, as she rose with the ◊A. Hymie smiled and dropped his ◊Q, but Rose's club return sank the contract as West was able to cash the ♣J after he got in with his ◊K.

DEAL 4. PROTECTING PARTNER'S ENTRY

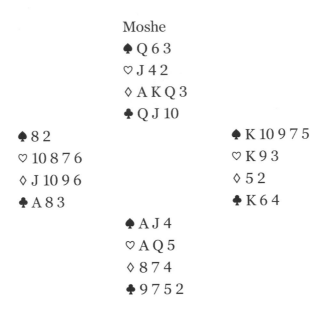

Moshe
♠ Q 6 3
♡ J 4 2
◇ A K Q 3
♣ Q J 10

♠ 8 2
♡ 10 8 7 6
◇ J 10 9 6
♣ A 8 3

♠ K 10 9 7 5
♡ K 9 3
◇ 5 2
♣ K 6 4

♠ A J 4
♡ A Q 5
◇ 8 7 4
♣ 9 7 5 2

Moshe did well to open 1◇ instead of a supposed "15-point" 1NT with his flat, quack-laden hand, but that did let East stick in a non-vul 1♠ overcall. South was happy to bid an invitational 2NT with his two spade stoppers. North was happy to accept the invitation.

Declarer gobbled up West's ♠8 opening lead with his ♠J and led the ♣2 towards dummy. West played low, and East captured dummy's ♣10 with the ♣K. Helpless to continue spades, East exited passively in clubs.

Three diamond tricks, and with the help of a heart finesse, two tricks in every other suit gave South the nine he needed for 3NT.

Moshe was not pleased. "Shoulda made an overtrick on a routine double squeeze," he said.

Who, if anyone, erred in the play?

Moshe was right about the missed squeeze, but the worst error was West's. In the other room, Rose was West. After the same start, she rose with her ♣A at Trick 2 to lead her last spade through dummy's remaining ♠Q6. Declarer won and drove out East's ♣K, but then East ran spades for down one.

14

DEAL 5. STEALING A TRICK OR
SAVING PARTNER'S ENTRY

```
                    ♠ 8 6 5
                    ♡ A K 9
                    ◇ Q J 5
                    ♣ Q J 10 9
♠ K 10 7 4 2                        ♠ J 9
♡ 10 7 5                           ♡ 8 6 3 2
◇ 9 8 4                            ◇ 7 6 3 2
♣ K 2                             ♣ A 7 5
                    ♠ A Q 3
                    ♡ Q J 4
                    ◇ A K 10
                    ♣ 8 6 4 3
```

South responded 3NT to North's 1♣. He had a spade tenace to protect and no four-card major to bid. West led the ♠4 to East's ♠J and declarer's ♠Q. He entered dummy in hearts to lead the ♣Q.

East let dummy's ♣Q ride and West won the ♣K. Knowing that declarer wouldn't bypass 1♠ with ♠AQ93, he pounded the ♠K to drive out declarer's ♠A. Not wanting to hear North complain about missed overtricks, South won the ♠A and led low to East's ♣A.

If East had a third spade to return, the defenders could have held declarer to contract, but South won an overtrick and his partner's applause.

How did declarer go down in the other room?

After winning the ♠Q at Trick 1, Hymie, South in the other room, led the ♣3, confident that Rose, *West*, would rise with an honor if she had one. She had one, but somehow the ♣2 fell out of her hand.

East won the ♣A and returned the ♠9. Rose overtook with the ♠10 to clear the suit. Soon she won the ♣K and two more spades. Down one, but East, Double-Dummy Doug, scolded her: "If you'd led your deuce of clubs, I'd have come through the spades and we'd have beaten him two."

"No," said Hymie, "but I don't think so."

DEAL 6. SECOND HAND LOW WHEN
YOU HAVE THE LONG SUIT

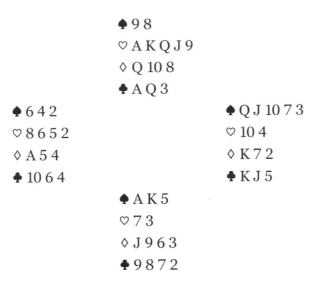

♠ 9 8
♡ A K Q J 9
♢ Q 10 8
♣ A Q 3

♠ 6 4 2
♡ 8 6 5 2
♢ A 5 4
♣ 10 6 4

♠ Q J 10 7 3
♡ 10 4
♢ K 7 2
♣ K J 5

♠ A K 5
♡ 7 3
♢ J 9 6 3
♣ 9 8 7 2

East's 1♠ overcall didn't keep South from responding 1NT, nor North from raising to 3NT. After winning the ♠A at Trick 1, declarer crossed to dummy in hearts to start diamonds with dummy's ♢Q. Hoping that West had the ♢J, East covered with the ♢K and continued with the ♠Q.

South as he ducked. East's ♠J fell to South's ♠K next, but after running hearts declarer led dummy's ♢10. West ducked and won dummy's ♢8 next to shift to clubs. But needing only one trick more, declarer put up dummy's ♣A at Trick 12. He lost one more trick, to East's ♣K at Trick 13.

How should the defense arrange to defeat 3 NT?

In the Open Room, East had forgotten that the defender with the long suit should retain his last outside entry until that suit is ready to roll, leaving it to the short defender to win earlier tricks.

In the Closed Room East ducked dummy's ♢Q. When West won the ♢A and continued spades, South ducked, but a third spade dislodged his ♠K.

Unable to establish a diamond trick without letting East in and in hand for the last time, South tried a desperate club finesse. Oops, down two. But yes, a better declarer could have squeeze-endplayed East.

DEAL 7. SECOND HAND HIGH TO PRESERVE TRANSPORTATION

```
                         ♠ Q 6
                         ♡ K 8 7 3
                         ◇ A K 10 7 3
                         ♣ 8 2
        ♠ A 9 7 4 3                        ♠ 8 5 2
        ♡ J 9 6                            ♡ Q 10 5
        ◇ 8                                ◇ Q 6 5 4
        ♣ J 9 4 3                          ♣ A 10 6
                         ♠ K J 10
                         ♡ A 4 2
                         ◇ J 9 2
                         ♣ K Q 7 5
```

North responded 1◇ to South's 1♣ and raised South's 1NT rebid to 3NT. Declarer won West's ♠4 opening lead with dummy's ♠Q to start clubs promptly. When his ♣K held, he reverted to diamonds.

Though his ◇J lost to East's ◇Q at Trick 3, his ♣K was allowed to hold Trick 4 and he scampered home with four diamonds to go with his early club trick and two tricks in each major. Making 3NT on the button.

Were two spade stoppers enough?

Not if East were wide awake. In the other room Hymie was West and Rose was East. The bidding and play to Trick 1 were the same, but Rose was aware of the threat dummy's diamonds posed.

When South led dummy's ♣2 to Trick 2, Rose pounced with her ♣A to lead the ♠8 through what she supposed might be declarer's remaining ♠AJ.

South falsecarded the ♠K, but Hymie remembered Rose's ♠2 at Trick 1 and realized that she had three spades. Though he ached to capture declarer's ♠K with his ♠A, reason prevailed over instinct. He managed to snatch the ♠3 from his left hand.

Needing to find a ninth trick somewhere, South tried a diamond finesse. Rose won and led her last spade to Hymie, who cashed the setting tricks.

DEAL 8. THE CONVENIENCE STORE COUP

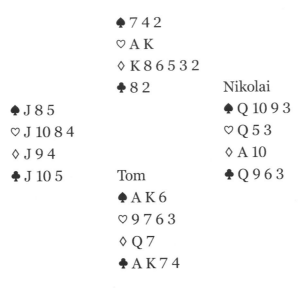

```
                    ♠ 7 4 2
                    ♡ A K
                    ◊ K 8 6 5 3 2
                    ♣ 8 2          Nikolai
    ♠ J 8 5                        ♠ Q 10 9 3
    ♡ J 10 8 4                     ♡ Q 5 3
    ◊ J 9 4                        ◊ A 10
    ♣ J 10 5        Tom            ♣ Q 9 6 3
                    ♠ A K 6
                    ♡ 9 7 6 3
                    ◊ Q 7
                    ♣ A K 7 4
```

West led the ♡J against 3NT. At Trick 2, declarer led to his ◊Q, which held. He tried his only hope, that the ◊A would swallow air on the second round. East won the ◊A and returned a heart to drive out dummy's ♡A, but it was too late. Declarer had 11 tricks. West won Trick 13 with the ♡10.

"Hmmm," said the kibitzer. "A rare Convenience Store Coup!"

What did he mean by that?

The play in the other room will make it clear. There East realized that his ◊A was doomed to swallow air, if not at Trick 2, then at Trick 3. He appreciated the urgency of killing dummy before the diamonds were ready to roll.

So he rose with the ◊A at Trick 2 and killed the dummy with a heart return. Now declarer had only seven tricks, unlike the declarer in the first room, who took eleven.

In the first room, declarer had turned 7 into 11, The Convenience Store Coup. "And who deserves the credit? Who deserves the blame?"

Danny blames Nikolai Ivanovich Lobachevsky, East in the first room, but Jim credits South, Tom Lehrer, for The Convenience Store Coup.

DEAL 9. TOUGH SECOND HAND HIGH TO PRESERVE PARTNER'S ENTRY

```
                        ♠ A 6 5
                        ♡ K J 9 8
                        ◊ A Q 7
                        ♣ 7 6 3
      ♠ Q 4                              ♠ J 10 9 8 2
      ♡ A 7 6 2                          ♡ Q 4
      ◊ 9 2                              ◊ J 10 6 5
      ♣ K 10 9 8 5                       ♣ 4 2
                        ♠ K 7 3
                        ♡ 10 5 3
                        ◊ K 8 4 3
                        ♣ A Q J
```

After a routine auction to 3NT, West led the ♣10. South took care to win Trick 1 with his ♣J, a known card, instead of the usual (for declarers) "higher of equals" ♣Q. Then he led the ◊3 to dummy's ◊Q to start hearts from dummy. Recognizing East as the Danger Hand, he was perfectly willing to lose a trick to West's ♡Q if she had it.

Neat! Had declarer started hearts in the usual way, floating his ♡10 at Trick 2, a loss to East's ♡Q could sink the contract.

How did the defense prevail in the other room against a similar play?

There South won Trick 1 with the ♣Q and crossed to dummy's ◊A, but East, Rose, was suspicious. In her girlhood, she had seen too many pickpockets roaming Second Avenue between Second and Houston Streets.

If declarer had the ♡A, with or without the ♡10, he was about to lead dummy's ♡8 and let it ride into the "safe" West hand. So Rose prepared to rise with her ♡Q at Trick 3 even before following to Trick 2.
When it held, her club return established the setting tricks in time.
Well done!

DEAL 10. SECOND HAND HIGH WITH ALL THE ENTRIES

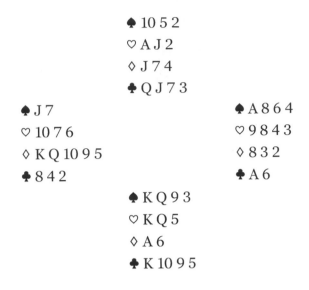

♠ 10 5 2
♡ A J 2
◊ J 7 4
♣ Q J 7 3

♠ J 7
♡ 10 7 6
◊ K Q 10 9 5
♣ 8 4 2

♠ A 8 6 4
♡ 9 8 4 3
◊ 8 3 2
♣ A 6

♠ K Q 9 3
♡ K Q 5
◊ A 6
♣ K 10 9 5

After opening a 15-to-17 HCP 1NT, South had more than enough to accept North's 2NT invitation. West led the ◊K, top of a broken sequence, against 3NT. East played the two, showing an odd number.

Declarer won the ◊A, crossed to dummy's ♡J, and led low to his ♠K. When it held, he knocked out East's ♠A. When East returned the ◊8, West read her for three and ducked to preserve his ◊Q as an entry. Dummy's ◊J gave declarer a second diamond trick to go with one spade and three tricks each in hearts and clubs. Nine tricks home with little sweat.

Could the defenders have won the race by taking five tricks first?

Yes. In the other room West led the ◊Q, a fancy opening lead to induce East to drop the ◊J under it if she had it. East, Rose, didn't have the ◊J, but she did have the habit of counting her partner's points at the start of play.

Reading West for at most the ♠J outside of diamonds, she rose with her black aces at every opportunity to lead diamonds. West knew to duck the second round, win the third, and cash two long diamonds to beat 3NT.

DEAL 11. IN FOR A PENNY, IN FOR A POUND

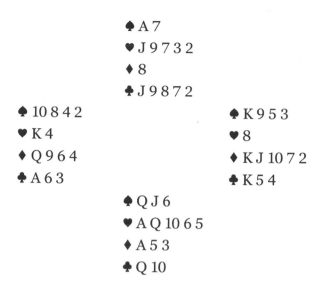

♠ A 7
♥ J 9 7 3 2
♦ 8
♣ J 9 8 7 2

♠ 10 8 4 2　　　　　　　♠ K 9 5 3
♥ K 4　　　　　　　　　♥ 8
♦ Q 9 6 4　　　　　　　 ♦ K J 10 7 2
♣ A 6 3　　　　　　　　　♣ K 5 4

♠ Q J 6
♥ A Q 10 6 5
♦ A 5 3
♣ Q 10

In second seat, despite minimal high-card strength 1NT opening, and East's lead-directing double, South super-accepted North's 2♦ transfer bid. Only adverse vulnerability kept West from saving in diamonds. In for a penny, in for a pound, North pushed on to 4♥.

South won the opening diamond lead. Eager to avoid a spade finesse, he led the ♣10 to Trick 2. West played low, East's ♣K won and East continued diamonds to tap dummy. A second club drove out West's ♣A, and West was able to lead a spade.

But South had read Dr J's book on Finesses and refused to finesse in either major. He cashed the ♥A hoping the ♥K might fall singleton. No but OK.

He discarded his ♠J on dummy's ♣J, and when West had to follow suit, South had time to discard the ♠Q on dummy's ♣9. West ruffed with the ♥K but by then, South was trump flush and made 4♥. Well declared!

Any way 4♥ could have been defeated?

Yes. In the other room the auction and opening lead were the same. But West, reading the position, played second hand high, grabbed his ♣A at Trick 2, and switched to the ♠8 in time to establish the setting trick.

DEAL 12. DIFFICULT SECOND HAND HIGH

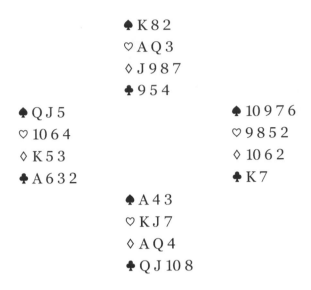

```
                      ♠ K 8 2
                      ♡ A Q 3
                      ◊ J 9 8 7
                      ♣ 9 5 4
    ♠ Q J 5                        ♠ 10 9 7 6
    ♡ 10 6 4                       ♡ 9 8 5 2
    ◊ K 5 3                        ◊ 10 6 2
    ♣ A 6 3 2                      ♣ K 7
                      ♠ A 4 3
                      ♡ K J 7
                      ◊ A Q 4
                      ♣ Q J 10 8
```

North's direct raise of 1NT to 3NT led West to lead a top-of-short-sequence ♠Q instead of a fourth-highest ♠2. East signaled with the ♠10 then ♠6 to encourage as declarer ducked the ♠Q and captured West's ♠J continuation with dummy's ♠K.

When declarer led dummy's ♣4 to Trick 3, East ducked smoothly. West won and led her last spade. East won the next club, and cashed the ♠9, the fourth trick for the defense.

When declarer's diamond finesse (his last hope) failed, so did 3NT.

Did declarer have a better shot?

Yes. In the other room, Rose, West also led the ♠Q. Hymie, South, ducked and won Rose's ♠J continuation in hand with the ♠A. He read East for the longer spades and thought to dislodge his likely club entry early.

Just as the defender with the length in his side's suit tries to save his entries for later, so also a good declarer tries to induce him to spend his entries early. Accordingly, Hymie tried to slip the ♣8 through West.

"Seriously" asked Rose? She took the ♣A, led her last spade to dummy's ♠K, and waited to take the setting trick with her ◊K later.

No swing!

DEAL 13. THE AGONY AND THE ECSTASY

```
                    ♠ 4 3 2
                    ♡ Q J 7 4
                    ◊ K 9 6
    Petula          ♣ J 8 5         Clark
    ♠ Q J 10 9 8 6                  ♠ A 7
    ♡ K                             ♡ A 9 8 6 2
    ◊ 10 7                          ◊ Q J 8 3 2
    ♣ 9 7 4 2                       ♣ 10
                    ♠ K 5
                    ♡ 10 5 3
                    ◊ A 5 4         Danny
                    ♣ A K Q 6 3
```

You may look askance at West's Weak 2♠ Bid as dealer, but please forgive Petula Pro. She had to shake things up a bit playing with Clark. South " balanced" with 2NT and North raised to 3NT.

Petula led the ♠Q. Clark had just learned Upside-Down Signals. Remembering "upside-down count," he played the ♠7 to show an even number ... or was he encouraging to show the ace? The *agony*!

After winning the ♠K, South cashed the ♣K and led low to dummy's ♣J next. Clark turned to Danny, whom he thought was kibitzing *him*, and beamed, "Aren't you proud of me? I ducked the first club to keep dummy's jack from becoming an entry!" as he tried to rake in this trick with the ♠A.

Petula reached out to clasp his hand, saying, "Not your trick!" The ecstasy! "Well, the jack *is* an entry and I know how to use it," said South. Desperate for a ninth trick, he pulled the ♡Q from dummy. "Always cover an honor with an honor," said Clark.

You can guess what he played. Pet, who had carefully followed to the previous two tricks was helpless as her ♡K fell beneath Clark's ♡A.
The final agony.

"I'm glad I'm a songwriter," said Danny. "I'm glad I'm a singer," said Pet.

DEAL 14. THE AGONY AND THE ECSTASY: PART TWO

```
                          ♠ 4 3 2
                          ♡ Q J 7 4
                          ◇ K 9 6
        Jim               ♣ J 8 5              Grace
        ♠ Q J 10 9 8 6                         ♠ A 7
        ♡ K                                    ♡ A 9 8 6 2
        ◇ 10 7                                 ◇ Q J 8 3 2
        ♣ 9 7 4 2                              ♣ 10
                          ♠ K 5
                          ♡ 10 5 3
                          ◇ A 5 4
                          ♣ A K Q 6 3
```

In the other room, Jim, West, was playing with Grace, an "advanced" beginner. He too opened a Weak 2♠ Bid as dealer. Here South doubled and bid 3NT over North's 3♡. Jim led the ♠Q. Grace ducked (the agony!), and South won the ♠K.

Declarer started clubs, cashing the ♣A then leading the ♣3 towards dummy. Jim followed first with the ♣9 and then with the ♣7, a high-low that in context showed a likely entry in the higher-ranking of the two unknown suits, hearts and diamonds.

Somehow, Grace realized she had blocked the spades and discarded the ♠A on the second club. Ah, the *ecstasy*: amazing Grace!

Seeing only eight tricks, after winning dummy's ♣J, in desperation declarer led the ♡Q from dummy. Grace was puzzled wondering which of Mother Goose's rhymes applied. Was it "Third hand high, second hand low!" or "Second hand high, third hand low!"? Who could remember?

Suddenly, Grace remembered the tie-breaker: "Always cover an honor with an honor!" Did the ace fall from Grace, or did Grace fall from grace? You guessed it: the same either way. The final *agony*.

Teaching bridge is a tough way to make a living.

"I'm glad I'm a radiologist," says Jim.

DEAL 15. JUMP, DON'T WAIT, TO COVER

```
                      ♠ 6 4
                      ♡ A 7 6
                      ◊ A Q J 7
                      ♣ Q J 9 3
      ♠ Q J 10 9 2                    ♠ 7 5 3
      ♡ Q 5 3 2                       ♡ J 10 8
      ◊ 10 9                          ◊ 8 6 4 3
      ♣ A 6                           ♣ K 8 7
                      ♠ A K 8
                      ♡ K 9 4
                      ◊ K 5 2
                      ♣ 10 5 4 2
```

5♣ would have had a better chance, but even after South opened 1♣ on his wretched four-card suit, 3NT was the inevitable final contract.

After capturing West's ♠Q opening lead with his ♠A, South led the ◊5 to dummy's ◊J. Then as though to finesse, he continued with the ♣J from dummy. East had been taught, "Wait till your last chance to cover an honor."

West won the ♣A and continued with the ♠9, bottom of his sequence. This time declarer ducked, but when he won the third spade and drove out East's ♣K he took the rest, as West's entry to the long spades was gone.

What should East have been thinking?

Waiting to cover the last honor is a fine guideline, but it's still only a guideline not a rule. And yes, West might have had a singleton ♣A, but if he did, it was hard to imagine how the defense was going to prevail.

In the other room, East looked at South's suspicious diamond "finesse" at Trick 2 with a jaundiced eye. He pounced upon declarer's still more suspicious lead of dummy's ♣3 next. When East's ♣K won, he continued spades, and with West still having the ♣A as an entry, declarer had to go down.

DEAL 16. SECOND HAND HIGH TO PREVENT A SECOND FINESSE

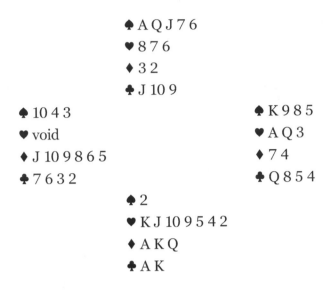

♠ A Q J 7 6
♥ 8 7 6
♦ 3 2
♣ J 10 9

♠ 10 4 3
♥ void
♦ J 10 9 8 6 5
♣ 7 6 3 2

♠ K 9 8 5
♥ A Q 3
♦ 7 4
♣ Q 8 5 4

♠ 2
♥ K J 10 9 5 4 2
♦ A K Q
♣ A K

South opened 2♣ and rebid 2♥ after North's 2♦ waiting bid. North bid 3♥, showing heart support and at least one outside ace or king. South bid 4♠, Kickback, a Key Card ask in hearts. North bid 4 NT showing one or four.

South could have asked for the trump queen by bidding 5♣, but knowing he had at least ten trumps, South bid 6♥. Hmm, not the dummy he was hoping for.

Declarer won the opening ♦J lead and played a spade to dummy, West playing the three. When declarer led a trump, Moshe followed low as did declarer.

When declarer led a second trump from dummy, the hand was over. Making six hearts. Lucky, lucky, said Stella, sitting West.

Lucky or poor defense?

At the other table, Second Hand Rose, sitting East was pretty sure from the play and carding that declarer had a singleton spade. When declarer led the first round of trumps, she jumped up with the ace and put declarer back in his hand.

With no way to reach dummy, declarer had a second trump loser.

DEAL 17. CAUTION: DEEP WATERS

```
                      ♠ J
                      ♡ Q 9 5
                      ◊ K 10 9 8 3
                      ♣ J 5 3 2
        ♠ K 9 8 5 3                    ♠ 10 7 4 2
        ♡ 6 4 3                        ♡ K J 10
        ◊ 7                            ◊ A 5 2
        ♣ K 9 8 4                      ♣ 10 7 6
                      ♠ A Q 6
                      ♡ A 8 7 2
                      ◊ Q J 6 4
                      ♣ A Q
```

After opening 1◊, South reached 3NT. He won West's ♠5 opening lead in dummy and led the ◊10 at Trick 2, as though he might be trying to take a finesse against a missing jack.

When the ◊10 won. He took a club finesse to his queen, losing to West's ♣K. West shifted to the ♡6, but this was too late. Declarer played low from dummy and captured East's ♡10 with his ace.

He drove out East's ◊A and finished with nine tricks: one heart, four diamonds, two spades, and two club tricks. Making 3 NT.

Did anyone do anything wrong?

In the other room, South also reached 3 NT, but Rose was again sitting East. She was suspicious when declarer led the ◊10. She hopped up with her ace to get another spade on the table. By the time South tried the club finesse he needed, West's spades had been established to take the setting tricks.

But both Souths erred. Had they finessed the ♣Q at Trick 2, South could keep East, the danger hand, off lead long enough to set up not only four diamonds but also the two club tricks he needed to get to nine on time.

PREVENTING

DECLARER

FROM

STEALING

DEAL 18. THAT OLD JACK TRICK

```
                        ♠ 8 4
                        ♡ A 10 9 8 4
                        ◇ J 4
                        ♣ J 5 3 2
        ♠ A Q 9 7 3                      ♠ J 10 2
        ♡ J 7 3                          ♡ K 5 2
        ◇ 8 3                            ◇ 9 6 5
        ♣ 10 9 6                         ♣ A 8 7 4
                        ♠ K 6 5
                        ♡ Q 6
                        ◇ A K Q 10 7 2
                        ♣ K Q
```

West led the ♠7 against South's 3NT. After capturing East's ♠10 with the ♠K, South crossed to dummy's ◇J to lead the ♣J. He wanted to appear as though he had ♣K109 and intended to finesse East for the ♣Q.

East didn't have the ♣Q so he played the ♣8, a count card, in tempo. However, it was the ♣A for which declarer was "finessing" East. South played the ♣K, then turned to West and begged, "My king, please stay off it!"

Of course South was joking, for he knew West didn't have the ♣A, else he'd have overcalled 1♠. West replied "Wouldn't dream of taking your king," and played the ♣6. South did not repeat this "finesse" but ran all the way home with one trick in each of the other suits to go with six diamond tricks.

How should the defense have proceeded?

In the other room, declarer tried the same ruse. However East jumped up with the club ace to get another spade on the table to sink the contract.

DEAL 19. SECOND HAND HIGH TO CASH YOUR TRICKS

```
                        ♠ Q 10
                        ♡ Q 10 3
                        ◇ K Q J 10 7
                        ♣ A K Q
        ♠ 9 8 7 6 3                      ♠ 5 4 2
        ♡ A 8 5                          ♡ K J 9 2
        ◇ 5 4 2                          ◇ A 8 6
        ♣ 4 2                            ♣ 7 5 3
                        ♠ A K J
                        ♡ 7 6 4
                        ◇ 9 3
                        ♣ J 10 9 8 6
```

South's 1NT response to 1◇ put West on lead after North raised to 3NT. West led the ♠9. Declarer won with dummy's ♠Q to preserve a spade entry to his hand. Then he unblocked dummy's clubs and tried the ◇7.

East covered gently with the ◇8, waiting to capture an honor with his ◇A. Oops, South won the ◇9 and took 9 tricks: three spades, one diamond, five clubs.

How should East have defended?

In the other room, play started the same. But Moshe was East and could almost see declarer's hand, having accounted for 9 HCP in South's black suits alone.

Picturing West with the ♡A and at least one other, he won the ◇A at his first opportunity and shifted to the ♡2. Four heart tricks and the ◇A meant down one.

DEAL 20. SECOND HAND HIGH TO CASH YOUR TRICKS

                        ♠ A 6 3
                        ♡ J 5 3
                        ◇ A 10 7 5 4
                        ♣ 9 8
        ♠ Q 9   ♠ J 8 5 2
        ♡ 10 8 6 4   ♡ A 7 2
        ◇ 6 3   ◇ 9 8 2
        ♣ A J 7 6 3   ♣ Q 10 5
                        ♠ K 10 7 4
                        ♡ K Q 9
                        ◇ K Q J
                        ♣ K 4 2

West led the ♣6 against the 1NT-2NT-3NT auction. East could count West for 7 HCP, and hoping they were the two top clubs, he played the ♣Q.

Declarer won the ♣K, crossed to dummy's ♠A, and led the ♡J. Hoping West's points included the ♡Q and declarer would misguess, East played the ♡2 in tempo.

Curtains! When the ♡J held Trick 3 and both defenders followed to the first diamond, South scurried home with five diamond tricks and the ♠K.

"How could you fall for that old jack of hearts trick?" asked West. "Didn't you learn the Rule of Eleven in Bridge 101?"

What was that about the "Rule of Eleven"?

In the other room, Rose was East. She knew the Rule of 11, which told her that the number of cards higher than West's spot-card lead held by the other three hands was 11 minus the rank of the card led.

Seeing four clubs higher than West's ♣6 in her hand and the dummy, she knew that declarer's ♣K was the lone high club that West didn't have. She placed West with ♣AJ76 and almost surely a fifth club, as leads from *four-card* suits headed by aces are good only when all other suits look worse.

She hopped right up with the ♡A to return the ♣10. West overtook and ran clubs to beat the contract.

DEAL 21. THAT OLD JACK TRICK AGAIN

```
                        ♠ 7 5 4
                        ♡ A 10 8 4
                        ◇ A Q 10
                        ♣ K 10 9
        ♠ Q J 10 6 3                      ♠ K 2
        ♡ 5 3 2                           ♡ 9 7 6
        ◇ J 4 2                           ◇ 7 6 5 3
        ♣ A 2          Moshe              ♣ 7 5 4 3
                        ♠ A 9 8
                        ♡ K Q J
                        ◇ K 9 8
                        ♣ Q J 8 6
```

When East saw the strong hand with which dummy had raised South's 16-to-18 HCP 1NT opening to 3NT, she saw little hope unless West had long, strong spades. She overtook his ♠Q opening lead with her ♠K. Moshe, South, ducked the ♠K but won East's ♠2 return with the ♠A.

He led the ♣J, West followed with the ♣2, perhaps thinking, "Here's another queen that Moshe will misguess."

When East followed with the ♣5, West asked, "Did you leave your queen in your handbag?" Before she could answer, Moshe claimed his contract with seven tricks in the red suits.

As he showed his cards, East countered, "Did you leave your abacus in your car, or did you think we were playing with a 42-point deck?

Huh? What did she mean by that?

Count the points. West could see 21 "4-3-2-1" points in his own hand and dummy, and East's ♠K at Trick 1 made 24. East could have no more than a jack left even if Moshe had shaded his 16-18 notrump by a point.

Did West need anything more to *beat the contract*?

DEAL 22. STOP, THIEF!

```
                        ♠ A K 5 3
                        ♡ 9 5
                        ◊ 5 2
                        ♣ A K Q 10 9
         ♠ Q J 9 6                      ♠ 8 4
         ♡ 7 4 2                        ♡ A J 10 3
         ◊ Q 10 8 6 3                   ◊ K 7 4
         ♣ 7          Arthur            ♣ 8 6 4 3
                        ♠ 10 7 2
                        ♡ K Q 8 6
                        ◊ A J 9
                        ♣ J 5 2
```

After passing as dealer and responding 1♡ to 1♣, South jumped to 2NT over North's 1♠ rebid. North bid 3NT. West led the ◊6.

South, Arthur Acecasher, was overjoyed to capture a king with his ◊A. Usually he played his aces on air

Arthur crossed to dummy in clubs to start hearts with dummy's ♡5. This time a king won the trick. Much as Arthur loves overtricks, he abandoned hearts and took the next six tricks in the black suits to make 3NT.

More of the same old, same old?

Yes, just another petty thief stealing a ninth trick. In the other room, Hymie, who was known in town as "the Honest Dutchman," didn't resort to theft. He ducked the first two diamonds, won the third, and eventually earned an overtrick by leading hearts from dummy twice.

No justice: only a 1-IMP pickup.

DEAL 23. SECOND HAND HIGH TO KEEP DECLARER FROM STEALING

```
                    ♠ 9 7
                    ♡ A 8 3
                    ◇ J 10 8 4
    Moshe           ♣ K Q J 2        Joe
    ♠ A Q 8 6 2                      ♠ J 10 5
    ♡ 9 7 5 2                        ♡ Q 10 6
    ◇ 9 7 5                          ◇ A 6 2
    ♣ 8               Petula          ♣ 9 7 6 4
                     ♠ K 4 3
                     ♡ K J 4
                     ◇ K Q 3
                     ♣ A 10 5 3
```

Against a routine 1NT-3NT auction, Moshe led the ♠6. Petula Pro captured Sleepy Joe's ♠10 with her ♠K. Unfortunately for Moshe, Petula knew Moshe's game too well, especially his aversion to leads from
four-card suits headed by aces.

Reading his spade holding almost exactly, she figured that driving out the defenders' ◇A would lead to immediate defeat. Desperately, she crossed to dummy in clubs to try that Old Jack Trick.

Joe played the ◇2 when Pet led the ◇J from dummy, but when West failed to win the ◇Q, he looked startled. Whereupon Pet changed horses, hooked the ♡J, and scampered home with nine tricks.

In the other room, an equally foxy South declared 3NT. How do you think he fared after the same spade lead?

Not so well. East knew from the Rule of 11 that West had the ♠A and ♠Q, but she was also counting the points and knew he could have no other queen.

When declarer tried the same ploy, she flew ◇A and shot back the ♠10. West overtook and ran the rest of the spades to beat 3NT.

DEAL 24. A CACOPHONY OF CONVENTIONS

♠ J 7 4 2
♡ K
♢ 6 2
♣ K Q 10 6 5 2

♠ 9
♡ Q J 10 3 2
♢ A Q 10 9
♣ 9 8 4

♠ A 8
♡ 8 7 6
♢ 8 7 5 4 3
♣ A 7 3

♠ K Q 10 6 5 3
♡ A 9 5 4
♢ K J
♣ J

After South's third-seat 1♠ opening, North bid 2♢, **Drury,** to show a four-card limit raise. South jumped to 4♠. Deterred by East's failure to double 2♢ for the lead, Arthur Acecasher refrained from indulging in his usual habit and led a mundane ♡Q instead.

At Trick 2, declarer called for dummy's ♠J. Hoping West could win a short ♠K, East ducked. Curtains! South overtook, ditched dummy's ♢2 on the ♡A and dislodged East's ♠A. East's ♢8 shift came too late.

Now declarer had only three losers and made 4♠.

Would you have been fooled by declarer's little ploy?

Not if you paused to wonder why West didn't lead diamonds. Don't ask how South made 4♠ in the other room after a different auction. An alert East could have hopped up with as ace in whichever black suit declarer led from dummy at Trick 2. Down one after a diamond shift.

We suspect, however, that after winning dummy's ♡K at Trick 1, South may have slipped dummy's ♣2 past a somnambulant East at Trick 2.

DEAL 25. ASLEEP AT THE SWITCH

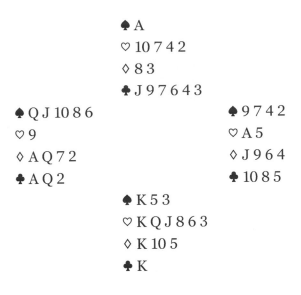

                ♠ A
                ♡ 10 7 4 2
                ◇ 8 3
                ♣ J 9 7 6 4 3

♠ Q J 10 8 6   ♠ 9 7 4 2
♡ 9   ♡ A 5
◇ A Q 7 2   ◇ J 9 6 4
♣ A Q 2   ♣ 10 8 5

                ♠ K 5 3
                ♡ K Q J 8 6 3
                ◇ K 10 5
                ♣ K

Some confusion whether North's 3♡ jump raise was invitational or weak over West's 1♠ overcall prodded South to bid an iffy 4♡.

After winning West's ♠Q opening lead in dummy, declarer led dummy's ♡10, as he would if he intended to finesse against a missing ♡Q.

Accordingly, East followed low. South won the ♡K and discarded a diamond from dummy on the ♠K. Goodbye, second diamond trick for the defenders, and hello game for declarer, who lost only one heart, one diamond, and one club.

Why should East win the first trump?

As the opening lead marked declarer with the ♠K, East was well placed to see a diamond discard coming … if he kept his eyes open. The danger of crashing partner's trump honor was merely conjectural, but the coming diamond discard was certain.

In the other room, East was wide awake, and won the first heart to shift to diamonds. Down one.

DEAL 26. SECOND HAND HIGH BEFORE DECLARER HAS NINE TRICKS

```
              ♠ 7 2
              ♡ 9 4
              ◊ 8 6 5 3
              ♣ A K Q J 10
♠ 9 8 6 5 4                ♠ J 10 3
♡ 8 6 5 3                  ♡ A 7 2
◊ A 10 4                   ◊ K J 9 2
♣ 3                        ♣ 9 6 2
              ♠ A K Q
              ♡ K Q J 10
              ◊ Q 7
              ♣ 8 7 5 4
```

After a simple 1NT-3NT auction, declarer won West's ♠9 opening lead with the ♠A. Guessing East for the ♡A, South crossed to dummy in clubs to lead towards his hearts.

Once East ducked, the rest didn't matter. Declarer won, abandoned hearts, and cashed out in the black suits to make his fragile contract.

West offered to buy East an alarm clock. "I'll accept only a Snooze-Alarm," replied East.

In the other room, East had imbibed two cups of coffee to keep herself awake. Once declarer chose to attack hearts at Trick 3, she saw that as little as one heart trick would give declarer the nine tricks he needed.

However, as little as ◊A74 in the West hand would provide the setting tricks first. So, up with the ♡A, out with the ◊2 and goodbye, Charlie!

DEAL 27. SECOND HAND HIGH VERSUS A SECOND SUIT

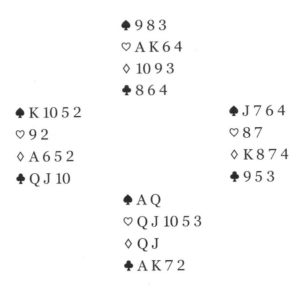

```
                        ♠ 9 8 3
                        ♡ A K 6 4
                        ◊ 10 9 3
                        ♣ 8 6 4
        ♠ K 10 5 2                  ♠ J 7 6 4
        ♡ 9 2                       ♡ 8 7
        ◊ A 6 5 2                   ◊ K 8 7 4
        ♣ Q J 10                    ♣ 9 5 3
                        ♠ A Q
                        ♡ Q J 10 5 3
                        ◊ Q J
                        ♣ A K 7 2
```

South needed no more encouragement than North's simple 2♡ raise to carry on to 4♡. After winning the opening club lead with his ♣A, he drew trumps with the ♡K and ♡Q.

Then he led the ◊Q to drive out the top diamonds and set up dummy's ◊10 for a spade discard to avoid a finesse.

Alas, West ducked this trick to East's ◊K and a spade shift set up West's ♠K for a fourth defensive trick before declarer could set up and take his nine. Down one.

How did the declarer in the other room earn a tenth trick?

With a little bit of guile to get him through. After the same auction and the same club lead, he won the ♣A, and crossed to the ♡K to lead dummy's ◊10.

Thinking to "wait for the last honor" to cover, East (the Danger Hand) played low. West won and continued clubs, but declarer was able to establish dummy's ◊9 for an eventual spade discard and ten easy tricks.

Making four hearts.

DEAL 28. SECOND HAND HIGH VERSUS A SECOND SUIT

♠ A J 4 2
♡ 7 6 5 3
◇ 8 4
♣ 8 6 3

♠ 7 5
♡ A Q 8
◇ Q 7 3
♣ Q 10 9 7 4

♠ 8 6 3
♡ K 10 4
◇ J 10 9 5 2
♣ 5 2

♠ K Q 10 9
♡ J 9 2
◇ A K 6
♣ A K J

After opening 2NT, South reached 4♠ via Stayman. Wary of blowing a trick in any of the three suits where his queens might take tricks if he waited with them, West led a passive trump.

Declarer had three fast heart losers and a club finesse. How could he avoid the club finesse? If hearts were 3-3, he could use to last heart to discard a club.

So he finished trumps ending in hand and exited in hearts, hoping to set up dummy's fourth heart. As West had discarded an encouraging ♣10, East overtook West's ♡8 with the ♡10 to shift to the ♣5.

South judged well to win the ♣A, and tried the ♡J, but East overtook West's ♡Q with the ♡K and declarer had nothing better than to finesse the ♣J. West won the ♣Q and prayed the ♡A would live. It did, and the contract died.

How did South in the other room set up dummy's fourth heart in time?

That declarer had read Dr J's book on Entries. After the same start, he won the third spade in dummy to start hearts. Now look at the defenders' tasks:

East must hop ♡K and West must unblock the ♡Q to have a chance, East did but West didn't. If West had dumped the ♡Q, South could counter by leading the ♡J after winning the club shift. Check and mate!

DEAL 29. SECOND HAND HIGH TO SWITCH SUITS

```
                        ♠ J 9 2
                        ♡ A Q 9
                        ◊ Q 8 7 3
                        ♣ A J 7
        ♠ K 6 3                         ♠ Q 10 7 5
        ♡ J 4 2                         ♡ 10 8 7 3
        ◊ A 9 5                         ◊ K 6 2
        ♣ 10 6 3 2                      ♣ 8 5
                        ♠ A 8 4
                        ♡ K 6 5
                        ◊ J 10 4
                        ♣ K Q 9 4
```

After North opened 1◊, South jumped to 3NT, ending the auction. West's ♣2 opening lead rode to South's ♣9. Needing only one diamond to come to nine tricks, South led an innocent ◊4 to Trick 2.

West covered with the ◊5. East captured dummy's ◊Q with his ◊K and shifting promptly to the ♠5.

Declarer ducked to West's ♠K and let East's ♠10 hold the next spade. Forced to win the third spade, he tried the ◊10 next. West ducked in hope that East had the ◊J, but having no more spades West could do no better by taking the ◊A at that point. Nine tricks rolled home.

Was either defender to blame for letting 3NT slip through?

Yes, West and West.
Second for failing to rise with the ◊A at Trick 2 to start spades, the most promising source of tricks for the defense, while East might still have a diamond entry.

But first for leading clubs, declarer's likely four-card suit, instead of spades, the stronger of West's three-card majors.
South's 3NT jump likely denied a four-card major. Therefore, West should think first to lead a major unless a minor-suit lead stands out.

DEAL 30. SECOND HAND HIGH TO SWITCH SUITS

```
                      ♠ 7 2
                      ♡ K 5 3
                      ◊ A J 8 7 6 3
                      ♣ 7 3
        ♠ 10 8 5                      ♠ A 9 6 4
        ♡ J 9 7 6 4                   ♡ Q 10
        ◊ 9 4                         ◊ K 2
        ♣ K 8 5                       ♣ Q J 9 6 4
                      ♠ K Q J 3
                      ♡ A 8 2
                      ◊ Q 10 5
                      ♣ A 10 2
```

In the Open Room, North and South were playing 16-to-18 HCP notrumps, so North gambled a 3NT raise, banking on the diamonds to come home.

Declarer saw that if West held the ◊K, he could come to nine tricks by finessing later, but if East held it, he'd need a spade trick. Accordingly, he won Trick 1 in dummy to lead the ♠2.

When his ♠K won, he changed horses and rode the ◊Q to initial defeat but ultimate victory. After winning East's heart return, he ran off five diamonds to go with the two hearts and one spade already taken, and the ♣A yet to come.

Could the defense have prevailed after the opening heart lead?

In the other room, a 15-17 HCP range fetched a 2NT raise, and South's hesitation before bidding 3NT marked him with 16 HCP exactly.

His play to Trick 1 marked him with the ♡A, and his choice to start spades at Trick 2 suggested strength there. The only chink in South's armor was thus clubs. The ♣K would give West the 4 HCP with which the North-South auction marked him.

Visualizing the deal almost exactly, Rose won the ♠A, shifted to the ♣Q, and continued with the ♣6 when it held. West, who had read Dr J's book on unblocking, dropped his ♣K under South's ♣A. Down *two*.

DEAL 31. DIFFICULT SECOND HAND
HIGH TO SAVE PARTNER'S ENTRY

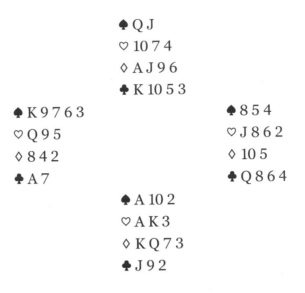

```
                      ♠ Q J
                      ♡ 10 7 4
                      ◊ A J 9 6
                      ♣ K 10 5 3
   ♠ K 9 7 6 3                        ♠ 8 5 4
   ♡ Q 9 5                            ♡ J 8 6 2
   ◊ 8 4 2                            ◊ 10 5
   ♣ A 7                             ♣ Q 8 6 4
                      ♠ A 10 2
                      ♡ A K 3
                      ◊ K Q 7 3
                      ♣ J 9 2
```

West led the ♠6 against South's 3NT contract. When dummy's ♠J won, declarer counted eight tricks and set about setting up a ninth in clubs.

Perceiving East as the Danger Hand, declarer chose to finesse through East. At Trick 2 he led the ♣3 to his ♣J. West won the ♣A, but could not continue spades without blowing a trick. After West shifted to diamonds, South had time to drive out East's ♣Q and set up a second club for an overtrick.

How did the defenders beat 3NT in the Closed Room?

After the same start, South finessed into the Danger Hand instead of through it. At Trick 2, he came to his hand with the ◊K and floated the ♣9. East won the ♣Q and returned the ♠8.

South ducked this to West's ♠K. He won West's spade return and had to go down when West got in with the ♣A to cash two long spades.
Should we credit South in the Open Room with deceptive play?

Maybe not. Actually it was the percentage play. South could finesse West for the ♣Q in either of two ways and chose the one that was better than 50%, succeeding not only when she was with West but also when she was with East and *slept in*.

DEAL 32. ONLY AN IMP

$\spadesuit$ 9 6 5 4
$\heartsuit$ 9 6
$\diamondsuit$ A Q J 10 9
$\clubsuit$ K 3

$\spadesuit$ Q 2
$\heartsuit$ 8 7 5 2
$\diamondsuit$ 5 4
$\clubsuit$ A 8 7 6 5

$\spadesuit$ A K J 10 7 3
$\heartsuit$ 10 3
$\diamondsuit$ 7 3
$\clubsuit$ Q 4 2

$\spadesuit$ 8
$\heartsuit$ A K Q J 4
$\diamondsuit$ K 8 6 2
$\clubsuit$ J 10 9

East dealt and opened a Weak 2$\spadesuit$ Bid. South overcalled 3$\heartsuit$ and confusion set in. North bid 4$\diamondsuit$, which South took as a fancy convention called "Last Train" agreeing hearts. He bid 4NT, intending it as an ask for key cards, only to sign off in 5$\heartsuit$ over North's one-key 5$\diamondsuit$ reply.

South ruffed the second spade, drew trumps and ran diamonds, only to find himself stranded in dummy in the all-club two-card ending:

$\clubsuit$ K 3

$\clubsuit$ A 7

$\clubsuit$ Q 4

$\clubsuit$ 10 9

East covered gently with the $\clubsuit$4, and South's cleverly concealed $\clubsuit$10 forced out West's $\clubsuit$A, letting declarer steal the fulfilling trick. Embarrassing, and sparing embarrassment for South, who could make 5$\heartsuit$ "legitimately" by playing West for two spades and the $\clubsuit$A, a virtual certainty on the auction.

Relief came when East and West compared scores at the end of the match. In the other room, East opened an under-strength 1$\spadesuit$. That left room
for the opponents to reach the cold 5$\diamondsuit$, which North made with an overtrick when East continued spades at Trick 2.

"Whew!" said East. "I blew only an IMP!"

Remember *Danny's Dictum: Always try to stop the opponents from winning Trick 12*. That's another occasion for *Second Hand High*.

DEAL 33. SECOND HAND HIGH TO
AVOID SWALLOWING AIR

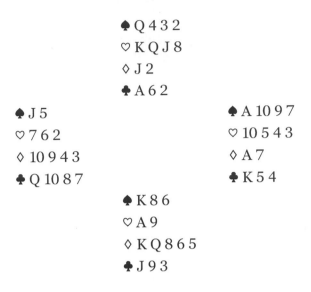

♠ Q 4 3 2
♡ K Q J 8
◇ J 2
♣ A 6 2

♠ J 5
♡ 7 6 2
◇ 10 9 4 3
♣ Q 10 8 7

♠ A 10 9 7
♡ 10 5 4 3
◇ A 7
♣ K 5 4

♠ K 8 6
♡ A 9
◇ K Q 8 6 5
♣ J 9 3

South opened 1◇ as dealer and rebid 1NT over North's 1♡ response. North raised to 3NT. With an easy choice between black suits, West led the ♣7. Declarer ducked Trick 1 to East's ♣K.

Declarer ducked again when East continued clubs. West covered the ♣9 with the ♣10. West's ♣8 drove out dummy's ♣A, whereupon declarer started diamonds with dummy's ◇J.

Hoping West might get in with the ◇Q to cash the ♣Q, East played low, but dummy's ◇J won. On the next lead from dummy, the ◇2, East's ◇A swallowed air. South had nine easy tricks: four in each red suit and the ♣A.

Could the defenders have taken five tricks first?

Yes. But not by letting his ◇A *swallow air*, capturing only a deuce. That didn't get him much bang for the buck. Look what would have happened if East had covered an honor, dummy's ◇J, with an honor, his ◇A.

In that event, South could get only two diamond tricks without letting West score the ◇10 and the thirteenth club. No way to come to the needed nine tricks from there. Might West have had a guarded ◇Q? Very unlikely, but taking the ◇A now wouldn't keep partner's ◇Q from scoring later.

DEAL 34. ACES ARE MEANT TO CAPTURE BIG GUYS

```
                          ♠ 9 6 5
                          ♡ J 2
                          ♢ A K Q J
                          ♣ Q 10 5 4
        ♠ 10 7 2                         ♠ J 8 3
        ♡ 10 9 8 4                       ♡ A 5
        ♢ 10 7                           ♢ 9 6 5 4 2
        ♣ K 8 2                          ♣ A 7 6
                          ♠ A K 4
                          ♡ K Q 7 6 3
                          ♢ 8 3
                          ♣ J 9 3
```

West appeared to have a normal safe ♡10 lead against 3NT, but his actual ♠2 lead was clearly right on this deal, as South had responded 1♡ to North's 1♢ opening.

South ducked the first spade, won the second, and crossed to the ♢J to start hearts with dummy's ♡J. Just a little extra chance in case hearts didn't split 3-3, for East might duck with a doubleton ♡A.

That's just what East had, and he did duck. When dummy's ♡J won, declarer continued with dummy's last heart. East's ♡A swallowed air.

Although East could have stopped an overtrick by leading the ♣A and another, he continued spades. Now declarer had ten easy tricks.

Could you make better use of your ace than drubbing a deuce?

In the other room, after the same start, declarer tried the same ploy, but Rose, East, sang out, "Better go back, Jack, do it again," and captured him with her ♡A.

When she continued spades, declarer could get only two heart tricks for a total of eight before the defenders got their five. Down one.

DEAL 35. PASSING TWO TESTS

         ♠ A Q J
         ♡ Q 5 3
         ◇ K 10 6
         ♣ J 10 5 3

♠ 9 4   ♠ 10 8 6 5 3
♡ A 9 8 7 4   ♡ K 10 6
◇ 9 8 5 3   ◇ 7 4
♣ 8 4   ♣ A 7 2

         ♠ K 7 2
         ♡ J 2
         ◇ A Q J 2
         ♣ K Q 9 6

West led a fourth-highest ♡7 against South's 3NT. We believe that a nine should be a weakness lead, denying as much as a queen in the suit.

East faced his first test at Trick 1 after declarer played low from dummy. The Rule of 11 told him that South had one heart higher than West's ♡7. If it were the ♡J or ♡A, either the ♡6 or the ♡10 would hold declarer to one heart trick. But if it were the ♡8 or ♡9, the ♡10 was the only card to keep declarer from winning any. So East played the ♡10, passing his first test.

Declarer won the ♡J and crossed to dummy's ♠J to lead the ♣J. Hoping it might fall to a ♣Q in his partner's hand, East played the ♣2. When the ♣J won, declarer rattled off four diamond tricks and two more spades for his nine-trick contract.

How could East have known enough to pass the second test?

Not "how" but *when*. Before turning his card to Trick 1, East in the other room made a mental note of West's exact holding. Her three hearts higher than the ♡7 could only be ♡A98, and with only four she could almost surely have found a better lead in some other suit.

The ♣Q would give her 6 HCP and the deck 41 HCP: first-grade arithmetic. So this East rose with the ♣A to play the ♡K and then the ♡6. West ran hearts to beat 3NT.

DEAL 36. SECOND HAND HIGH AGAINST
A DECEPTIVE DECLARER

           ♠ J
           ♡ Q J 7 2
           ◊ K Q 8 2
           ♣ A K 9 5

♠ A 10 7 6 4   ♠ 9 5 2
♡ A K 3   ♡ 10 9 4
◊ A 9 6   ◊ J 7 5
♣ 10 4   ♣ Q 8 7 6

           ♠ K Q 8 3
           ♡ 8 6 5
           ◊ 10 4 3
           ♣ J 3 2

South's 1NT reply to North's double of 1♠ falls short of the standard 8-10 HCP range, but we can all sympathize with his aversion to a 2♣ advance. North's 2NT raise pushed the envelope only slightly, and South was content to pass.

Dummy's singleton ♠J proved surprisingly valuable, as it held Trick 1 when West led the ♠6, but prospects for eight tricks looked dim.

To take advantage of his sparse resources, declarer led low towards his ◊10 at Trick 2. East played low but West captured the ◊10 with the ◊A.

Unsure how to continue, West shifted to the ♣10. East won the ♣Q and returned the ♣9. West captured South's ♣Q with the ♣A. South now had two spades, three diamonds, and three clubs. You could see the surprised look on his face.

How should the defenders have taken all their tricks?

In the Closed Room, Moshe, East, showed how. His ◊J was likely to be worthless unless West had the ◊A, so he rose with it when South at this table tried the same ploy as in the Open Room.

The "rule" for defenders is normally to return the higher of two remaining cards, but Moshe returned his low spade, retaining the ♠9. Joshua captured South's ♠K with the ♠A and continued with the ♠4.

Declarer captured Moshe's ♠9 with the ♠Q, but the defenders scored three spades, two diamonds, and two hearts. Down two!

DEAL 37. HOW TO PRESERVE TRANSPORTATION

```
                        ♠ K J 8 7 6
                        ♡ A 10 8 6
                        ◊ A 5
        Rose            ♣ 10 4        Hymie
        ♠ A 9 5                       ♠ 10 4 2
        ♡ Q 7 3 2                     ♡ J 4
        ◊ 8 4 2                       ◊ K 9 7 6 3
        ♣ J 6 2         Millie        ♣ A 7 3
                        ♠ Q 3
                        ♡ K 9 5
                        ◊ Q J 10      Danny
                        ♣ K Q 9 8 5
```

Rose led a "top of nothing" ◊8, the only unbid suit, against South's 3NT. Declarer ducked the first trick to East's ◊K and won East's ◊6 return with dummy's ◊A.

When South led the ♣10 from dummy and East unhesitatingly played low, South won the ♣K and led the ♠Q. Rose won the ♠A and drove out South's last diamond stopper, but declarer had nine tricks. Four spades, two hearts, two diamonds and one club.

Who deserves the credit? Who deserves the blame?

Danny, Southeast, smiled and shook his finger at East, saying, "You're a mean man, Hymie. Why don't you let Millie win her finesses once in a while?"

In the other room, Sid Signuller was East and did just that. He overtook West's ◊8 with his ◊9 to suggest a continuation and looked very disappointed to see South win with the ◊10.

South started spades with the ♠Q, but West continued with the ◊4 to drive out dummy's ◊A. Declarer won four tricks in spades and two in each red suit, but Sid took the setting tricks with the ♣A and ◊K73 in the end.

DEAL 38. SECOND HAND HIGH?
TAKE THE SETTING TRICK

```
              ♠ K 9 5
              ♡ Q J 2
              ◇ J 3
              ♣ A Q 8 6 5      Matt
  ♠ Q J 10 8                   ♠ A 4 3
  ♡ 6                          ♡ 10 7
  ◇ 10 7 6 4 2                 ◇ A 9 8 5
  ♣ J 9 3                      ♣ K 10 7 2
              ♠ 7 6 2
              ♡ A K 9 8 5 4 3
              ◇ K Q
              ♣ 4
```

South did well to stop in game after North made a game-forcing 2♣ response to his 1♡ opening, but even 4♡ was in jeopardy when West led the ♠Q.

The declarer ducked twice and East won the third spade. Since East had the club suit well stopped, he exited with a trump. Declarer won in dummy and led the diamond jack. East played low, hoping for a two-trick set.

Declarer won the king and cashed all his trumps. With two cards left, the position was: North: ♦ --- ♣ A Q
Poor East had to discard from ♦ A ♣ K 10
South: ♦ Q ♣ 4

Declarer took the last two tricks as East discarded the diamond ace, hoping partner had the diamond queen.
Making four hearts

What is the moral of this sad story?

Second hand high when it's the setting trick can't be terrible. In the other room, the defense took the first four tricks. Down one quickly.

DEAL 39. ON THE OTHER HAND

```
                    ♠ Q 10 8 6 4
                    ♡ A 7 4
                    ◇ A 7 3
                    ♣ J 2
    ♠ A 9 3                          ♠ K 7 2
    ♡ Q J 10 5                       ♡ 9 6 2
    ◇ 10 2                           ◇ K J 5
    ♣ 9 5 4 3                        ♣ Q 10 7 6
                    ♠ J 5
                    ♡ K 8 3
                    ◇ Q 9 8 6 4      Danny
                    ♣ A K 8
```

North scrounged up a simple invitational raise to 2NT over South's 1NT rebid, but with little more than a bare minimum, South wisely declined.

West led the ♡Q to dummy's ♡A. Declarer cashed dummy's ◇A and continued with dummy's ◇3. East rose ◇K and continued hearts, but declarer promptly took his eight tricks.

Was there any way for the defense to prevail?

Perhaps. In the other room, play started similarly, but when declarer led the second diamond, East played the ◇J. Declarer had to guess. Had West started with ◇ K2 and East with ◇ J105? If so, he needed to play low.

Jim had to leave early before he found out what happened. Danny had been kibitzing but did not hang around for the score comparison. For all we know, South in the Closed Room is still flipping a mental coin.

However, South *should* play the ◇Q. Some call it "Restricted Choice." The odds are nearly 2-to-1 that East *doesn't* have the touching honor. But it's also right for East to play the ◇J or ◇10 roughly at random when he has both; never the ◇K if he has another. Give South a chance to misguess!

KILLING

THE

DUMMY

DEAL 40. KILLING THE DUMMY
AND CREATING AN ENTRY

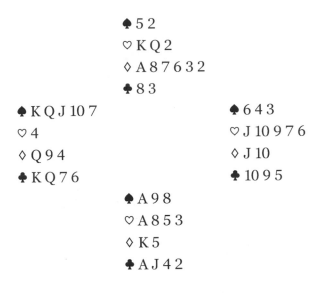

```
                    ♠ 5 2
                    ♡ K Q 2
                    ◊ A 8 7 6 3 2
                    ♣ 8 3
    ♠ K Q J 10 7              ♠ 6 4 3
    ♡ 4                       ♡ J 10 9 7 6
    ◊ Q 9 4                   ◊ J 10
    ♣ K Q 7 6                 ♣ 10 9 5
                    ♠ A 9 8
                    ♡ A 8 5 3
                    ◊ K 5
                    ♣ A J 4 2
```

North and South were playing the Lebensohl convention. That let North raise 1NT to 3NT while denying a stopper in overcaller's spade suit.

South ducked the first two rounds of spades and discarded dummy's ♣3 on the third spade, which he won. Then he cashed the ◊K and led the ◊5, ducking in dummy when West followed with the ◊4 and ◊9.

Hoping East had at least one diamond honor, South play low from dummy. East won, but had no way to reach West, so declarer took the rest.

How did the defense prevail in the other room?

Over Rose's 2♠ overcall, North bid 3♣, which was alerted as showing diamonds. After Moshe bid 3◊, North's 3NT asked Moshe to pass if he had a spade stopper.

Moshe won the third spade, but he led the ◊5 to Trick 4. "This lady is for burning," said Rose, plunking the ◊Q on the table. Moshe took dummy's ◊A and his own ◊K, but when he returned to dummy in hearts to lead another diamond, Rose won the ◊9.

"Curse of Scotland!" cried Flora McKenzie, East, who laughed while Rose ran the rest of the spades to beat poor Moshe.

DEAL 41. KILLING THE DUMMY

```
                        ♠ 7 6
                        ♡ Q 7
                        ◊ A J 10 8 7 5
                        ♣ 10 8 6
        ♠ J 9 5 3                       ♠ K 10 8 2
        ♡ 10 9 8 2                      ♡ K 6 5 4
        ◊ K 4                           ◊ Q 6 3
        ♣ J 9 2                         ♣ Q 4
                        ♠ A Q 4
                        ♡ A J 3
                        ◊ 9 2
                        ♣ A K 7 5 3
```

South had ample values for 3NT over North's non-vul Weak 2◊ Bid. Hoping West's ♡10 opening lead might be top of an internal sequence, he tried dummy's ♡Q, which fetched the ♡K from East.

After winning the ♡A, South floated the ◊9 to East's ◊Q, won East's heart return and when West's ◊K popped up on his next diamond lead, South took the rest, as the diamonds pseudo-squeezed West. Three overtricks!

"Should I have raised you to six?" asked North, apparently in earnest.
"Just be thankful I could make three," replied South.

How many tricks did the 3NT declarer take in the other room?

Not quite as many. Reaching 3NT, he received the same heart lead. But Rose, East, played second hand high, covering his ◊9 with her ◊K.
South might have won the ◊A and worked on clubs, but instead he ducked in dummy, won the heart return and finessed the ◊J next.

Oops! Eventually, he was able to set up two long club tricks, but he took only eight tricks in all, even with the ♠K on side.

DEAL 42. WHEN YOU ARE THE DANGER HAND

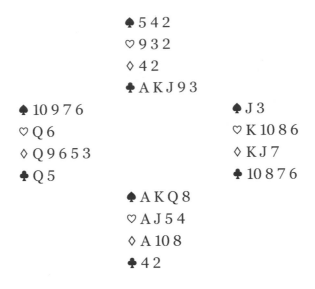

West led the ◊5 against 3NT. Declarer let East win the first two diamonds and discarded dummy's ♠2 on the third. South's deep-finesse

of dummy's ♣9 lost to East's ♣10.

East led the ♡10. South won the ♡A and led his last club. When West's ♣Q appeared, declarer struck his forehead with his right palm and cried, "Dummkopf! I should've finessed the jack on the first round." Then he ran off seven black-suit winners to go with his two red aces and made 3NT.

Will the real dummkopf please sign in?

Play started the same in the other room, but West had read Danny's book on *Sorting One's Cards*. He winked at his kibitzer and slyly mixed the ♣5 in with his spades.

When South led a club to Trick 4, West played the ♣Q. Winning dummy's ♣K, declarer continued with dummy's ♣A and turned to West, saying, "I hope that queen wasn't singleton."

"Oops," said West when his turn came. He struck his forehead and mumbled, "Dummkopf! What was this card doing among my spades? Sorry, pard," as he played the ♣5.

However, now South scored only three club tricks. Down one.

Oh yes, the real dummkopf was West in the first room. Had he followed to the first club with the ♣Q, South would have been helpless.

DEAL 43. FRERE JACQUES

```
                    ♠ 9 8 3
                    ♡ 9 6
                    ◇ A 5 3 2
                    ♣ A Q 9 4        Jacques
        ♠ J 10 5                     ♠ A 7 6 4
        ♡ A 10 8 7 2                 ♡ Q J 3
        ◇ 10 4                       ◇ Q J 9 8 7
        ♣ 8 6 3                      ♣ 2
                    ♠ K Q 2
                    ♡ K 5 4
                    ◇ K 6
                    ♣ K J 10 7 5
```

Against 3NT, West led a fourth-highest ♡7. South captured East's ♡J with the ♡K and entered dummy with the ♣Q. When he led the ♠9. East gave count with the ♠7, and declarer won the ♠K.

Forgetting that they were playing IMPs, South crossed to dummy's ◇A to lead the ♠3, winning the ♠Q this time. Then he ran off four more clubs and the ◇K before surrendering the last three tricks.

Tearfully, West asked East, "Jacques, dormez vous?"

In the other room, East was wide awake. When the ♡7 hit the table at Trick 1, she applied the Rule of 14: subtracting the rank of the spot-card from 14, she counted 7 hearts higher. She saw three of them in the dummy and her own hand, and playing "fourth highest" spot-card leads, she placed West with another three.

That left declarer with only one, surely the ♡A or ♡K, for the auction marked West with at most 5 HCP. As South's lone heart honor was gone, the suit would run, so East stepped up with her ♠A as soon as declarer led a spade from dummy. *Voila*, down one!

If you use fourth-highest leads, the Rule of 14 implies the Rule of 11,
a special case thereof. However, if you use third-highest, it's a Rule of 12 or fifth-highest, a Rule of 10. "Third and low"? Help! Aren't you glad you lead fourth-highest and can use a simple Rule of 11?

DEAL 44. BLOCKING THE DUMMY

```
              ♠ 8 5 2
              ♡ 6
              ◊ A 10 9 8 7 5 3
              ♣ 10 5
♠ J 10 3                        ♠ Q 9 6
♡ Q 10                         ♡ K 9 8 7 3
◊ K 2                          ◊ 6 4
♣ A J 9 7 3 2                  ♣ Q 8 6
              ♠ A K 7 4
              ♡ A J 5 4 2
              ◊ Q J
              ♣ K 4
```

North's 3◊ opening may not be everyone's cup of tea, but these days most would bid it. South converted to the "obvious" 3NT.

West led the ♣7 and declarer captured East's ♣Q with the ♣K. Fearing blockage in the diamond suit, South led a slightly deceptive ◊J. Hoping that East had the ◊Q, West played the ◊2. Whereupon South led the ◊J ride, When it held, declarer ran off the first 11 tricks.

How did West defend in the other room?

There Stella by Starlight wound up declaring 3NT. Like South in the Open Room she tried to slip the ◊J through after winning the ♣K at Trick 1.

Rose was West and she covered with the ◊K. Stella let it hold (her only chance, albeit wafer thin) and watched helplessly as Rose rattled off five club tricks. Down two.

Stella said "Lucky, lucky! You might have smothered a singleton queen in your partner's hand."

Was Stella right?

Yes. The only layout to which the ◊K catered was the actual one. The ◊K could lose not only if East had singleton ◊Q but also if Stella had ◊QJx or ◊QJxx and had planned to try to drop a singleton ◊K offside.

It's not always right to play "Second Hand High," even when it works.

DEAL 45. KILLING THE DUMMY

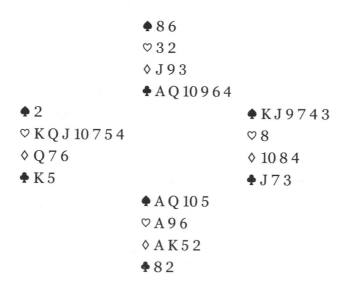

```
                      ♠ 8 6
                      ♡ 3 2
                      ◊ J 9 3
                      ♣ A Q 10 9 6 4
      ♠ 2                             ♠ K J 9 7 4 3
      ♡ K Q J 10 7 5 4                ♡ 8
      ◊ Q 7 6                         ◊ 10 8 4
      ♣ K 5                           ♣ J 7 3
                      ♠ A Q 10 5
                      ♡ A 9 6
                      ◊ A K 5 2
                      ♣ 8 2
```

South opened 1NT. West might have tried a "Hamilton" 2♣ to show an unspecified suit, but he bid 3♡ instead, a Weak Jump Overcalls. North gambled 3NT despite his lack of a heart stopper.

Declarer ducked West's ♡K opening lead but captured his ♡10 continuation with the ♡A. Then he deep-finessed the ♣9. East won the ♣J and shifted to the ♠9. Declarer won the ♠A, refusing the risky finesse, and took his nine tricks when West's ♣K popped up on the next club lead.

How did the defense prevail in the other room?

The play to Tricks 1 and 2 was the same. It was at Trick 3 that the play deviated: West put up the ♣K. Declarer had no choice but to win dummy's ♣A.

Looking at all four hands, you might think to use dummy's two club entries to double-finesse spades, then stick West in with a heart and judge to play him for the ◊Q in the resulting three-card ending.

However, the actual declarer cashed dummy's ♣Q next, hoping the ♣J would fall. When it didn't, the contract was doomed.

Rising with a short king is usually right when dummy's strong suit lies behind him like a guillotine. That gives declarer many ways to go wrong, and a king who hangs back from battle will soon be dead anyway.

DEAL 46. SECOND HAND HIGH FROM A DANGER HAND

```
                    ♠ A K 10 9 5
                    ♡ Q 9 5
                    ♢ 8 7 5
                    ♣ 7 3
      ♠ Q 8 4                        ♠ J 7 6
      ♡ J 6                          ♡ K 10 8 7 3 2
      ♢ Q J 3                        ♢ 9 4 2
      ♣ Q 10 9 8 5    Millie         ♣ 6
                    ♠ 3 2
                    ♡ A 4
                    ♢ A K 10 6
                    ♣ A K J 4 2
```

Open 1♣, hope partner doesn't pass, and then "reverse" into 2♢? Maybe, but Thoroughly Modern Millie opened 2NT in second seat with her 5+ Honor Tricks. That led to a lead-directing double of a 3♡ transfer bid, a wrong-sided 3NT, and an unpleasant ♡J opening lead.

All four top hearts went on Trick 1. Millie led the ♠2 to Trick 2 and inserted dummy's ♠9 when West followed low. East won the ♠J, but dummy's remaining ♡95 stood guard, so East could not run the hearts.
A 3-3 spade split let Millie bring nine tricks home without need of any luck in a minor suit.

Was a successful defense possible?

Rose, West in the other room, showed that it was. When Uncle Walter, declaring 3NT after the same auction, led the ♠2 to Trick 2, Rose played the ♠Q. "Does that mean you have the jack of diamonds too?" asked Walter.

Uncle Walter took his two top tricks in spades, clubs and diamonds, then conceded down two when no more queens fell.

Eddie Kantar says, "Declarers hate defenders who do this." Don't mind Eddie. He'd hate his grandma if she made good plays against him.

DEAL 47. KILLING DUMMY'S SUIT

```
                    ♠ 6 5 3
                    ♡ 7 2
                    ◇ 8 5 4
                    ♣ A J 10 9 8
    ♠ Q J 10 9 8                  ♠ 7 4 2
    ♡ K 10 9 5                    ♡ Q 8 3
    ◇ 6 2                         ◇ J 10 9 7
    ♣ K 4          Millie         ♣ Q 5 2
                    ♠ A K
                    ♡ A J 6 4
                    ◇ A K Q 3
                    ♣ 7 6 3
```

Millie opened 2NT again, this time with a more orthodox hand, and declared 3NT on the lead of the ♠Q. She had seven top tricks.

At Trick 2, she led to dummy's ♣8, losing to East's ♣Q. Upon winning the spade return, she led another club. When the ♣K popped up, she had ten tricks.

"Partner, we just went over this on the previous deal," moaned East.

To what was East referring? How could the defense have prevailed?

Yes, the previous deal featured sauce for the goose, West's ♠Q. This deal featured sauce for the gander, West's ♣K. There the monarch's sex mattered little; ♠K from ♠K84 in front of ♠AQ1095 would be right too.

In the other room, Rose was West. She played the ♣K on the first club. Declarer might have let her ♣K win, playing her for ♣KQx, but relying on "Restricted Choice" he took dummy's ♣A and continued with the ♣J.

When that held, he tried diamonds, hoping for a 3-3 split, but the actual 4-2 split left him one trick short.

Here the sex of the monarch matters. Rising with a doubleton queen *may* be just as effective but not always. Declarer may have the king and intend to win dummy's ace, then finesse on the way back. The "fair sex" often does need protection.

59

DEAL 48. KILLING DUMMY EVEN WITH ONLY A JACK

```
                        ♠ 7 5 4
                        ♡ 7 3
                        ◇ A K 10 9 6 2
                        ♣ 6 2
        ♠ Q 10 2                        ♠ J 9 3
        ♡ K Q J 10 6                    ♡ 8 5 4
        ◇ J 5                           ◇ Q 7 3
        ♣ 9 8 5                         ♣ Q J 10 7
                        ♠ A K 8 6
                        ♡ A 9 2
                        ◇ 8 4
                        ♣ A K 4 3
```

South reached 3NT. He ducked twice when West led the ♡K and continued with the ♡10. West's ♡Q then dislodged South's ♡A.

Declarer led a diamond to dummy's ◇9, which lost to East's ◇Q. As East had no more hearts, South soon claimed the rest. Overtrick!

"Not again, partner," sobbed East as she recorded minus 430.

"But this time I had only a jack," retorted West. "Not even a member of the royal family, and barely strong enough to lift my car when I get a flat."

How should we rate West's excuse?

Lame, and lacking the necessary signature from his mother. Didn't he once try "The brontosaurus ate my homework"?

West in the other room did not worship royalty. He knew that any card that forces a high card from dummy will suffice. Even a ten from 104 in front of dummy's AK9763 can help when declarer leads a deuce.

This West played the ◇J. Declarer could not duck lest West cash his hearts. Declarer won the diamond and reentering his hand with a club. South then lost a finesse to East's ◇Q. He took one diamond trick instead of five. Three undertricks instead of one overtrick.

DEAL 49. SECOND HAND HIGH TO KILL DUMMY

```
                        ♠ Q 7
                        ♡ 6 5
                        ◊ A Q 10 8 5 4
                        ♣ Q 10 3
        ♠ J 10 9 8 6                    ♠ A 5 2
        ♡ Q 10 7 3                      ♡ 8 4 2
        ◊ K 2                           ◊ J 9 6
        ♣ K 5                           ♣ 8 7 6 2
                        ♠ K 4 3
                        ♡ A K J 9
                        ◊ 7 3
                        ♣ A J 9 4
```

North's Weak 2◊ Bid led to a routine 3NT. West led the ♠J, declare played dummy's ♠Q and East won the ♠A. East returned the ♠5 to West's ♠8 as South ducked. Then West's ♠6 forced South's ♠K.

South deep-finessed dummy's ◊10, losing to East's ◊J. With no spade left, East shifted to clubs, but South rose with his ♣A.

When West's doomed ◊K fell on the next trick, declarer had five diamonds, two black-suit tricks, and two heart tricks coming. An automatic Sergeant Pepper Squeeze produced an overtrick.

Could the defense have done better?

In the other room, West rose with the ◊K on the first round. South took his best shot, taking dummy's ◊A and ◊Q before trying a club finesse.

West won the ♣K and cashed two more spades for down one.

PREVENTING

RUFFING

FINESSES

DEAL 50. WHEN A RUFFING FINESSE LOOMS

```
              ♠ A 8 7 4 3
              ♡ Q 5
              ◇ 9 8 7 4
Walter        ♣ Q 2
♠ 5                         ♠ 10
♡ K J 10 6 4 2              ♡ 9 8 3
◇ K 5                       ◇ A J 10 6 3 2
♣ A J 6 5                   ♣ K 4 3
              ♠ K Q J 9 6 2
              ♡ A 7
              ◇ Q
              ♣ 10 9 8 7
```

The auction began with East's Weak 2◇ Bid, South's 2♠ overcall, West's 3♡ response, and ended with North's "premature save" of 4♠.

West led the ◇K, then the ◇5. South ruffed, drew trumps with dummy's ♠A, and set about to establish his club side suit, such as it was. Figuring East for the shorter clubs, he led the ♣2 from dummy.

East played the ♣3 and West captured the ten with his ♣J. Uncle Walter reasoned that declarer would not have let him win a cheap trick with the ♣J when holding the ♣K, so he returned the ♣5.

South won East's ♡9 shift with the ♡A and led the ♣7. Uncle Walter ducked smoothly but declarer discarded dummy's ♡Q and soon claimed the rest. The "premature" 4♠ save turned into a *make*.

How could the defenders have beaten 4♠?

Not easily. Since declarer's strong club spot-cards were hidden from sight, it was hard for East to see the ruffing finesse coming.

However, East might have seen the need to step up with the ♣K at his first opportunity, in order to lead the ♡9 through declarer. West couldn't break hearts safely himself. If South had the ♣A and ♣J, East's ♣K was toast anyhow.

DEAL 51. AVOIDING A RUFFING FINESSE

```
                        ♠ 7 6 2
                        ♡ Q 10 9 6 3
                        ◇ Q 6
                        ♣ Q 10 5
        ♠ K 9 4                        ♠ Q J 10 5
        ♡ 8 7                          ♡ 5
        ◇ J 10 9 7                     ◇ K 3 2
        ♣ A 8 6 3                      ♣ K 9 7 4 2
                        ♠ A 8 3
                        ♡ A K J 4 2
                        ◇ A 8 5 4
                        ♣ J
```

Declaring 4♡ on an uncontested auction, South covered West's ◇J opening lead with dummy's ◇Q and captured East's ◇K with the ◇A. He crossed to dummy's ♡9 and led the ♣5 intending to finesse, but was startled to see his ♣J lose to West's ♣A.

He regained his composure and put his ♠A back with his spades where it belonged. West cashed the ◇9 before exiting safely with his last trump.

South won in dummy and led dummy's ♣Q. East covered with the ♣K but South ruffed. He returned to dummy with a diamond ruff and discarded the ♠3 on the ♣10. Losing one trick in each suit but trumps to make 4♡.

How did the defenders defeat the same contract in the other room?

A difficult defense! Had declarer started clubs from his hand, the defense would have been easy. East had to win the ♣K to avoid a ruffing finesse, then shift to spades to prevent a loser on loser play in clubs.

Jim refuses to identify the East who found the killing defense, and Danny refuses to believe it could be anyone but Eddie Kantar or ... nah, it couldn't have been ... Chthonic.

DEAL 52. AVOID THAT RUFFING FINESSE

<pre>
                      ♠ A K 9
                      ♡ Q J 10 7 3
                      ◇ 8 6 4
                      ♣ 5 4
      ♠ 6 5   ♠ 4 2
      ♡ A 6 5 2   ♡ K 8 4
      ◇ J 10 9 7   ◇ Q 5 3 2
      ♣ K J 8   ♣ 10 9 6 3
                      ♠ Q J 10 8 7 3
                      ♡ 9
                      ◇ A K
                      ♣ A Q 7 2
</pre>

South's pushy 6♠ slam seemed to hinge on a club finesse. But did it?

West led the ◇J. South won the ◇A, crossed to dummy's ♠K, and led the ♡3 to his ♡9. West won the ♡A and continued with the ◇9.

South won the ◇K, overtook the ♠Q with dummy's ♠A, and led dummy's ♡Q. Now declarer had a ruffing finesse position against East. She ruffed East's ♡K, and still had the ♠8 to lead to dummy's ♠9, the entry he needed to run the rest of dummy's hearts and discard clubs.

"How many times must you see this to get it right?" asked West.

To what was West referring? What could East have done better?

In the other room, East figured her ♡K was a goner if South had the ♡A. She played the ♡K on the first heart and shifted to clubs. Down one!

DEAL 53. AVOIDING ANOTHER RUFFING FINESSE

♠ K
♡ J 8 4 2
◇ A K 10 8
♣ Q 10 5 2

♠ J 10 4 3   ♠ Q 8 7 5 2
♡ 7   ♡ A K
◇ 6 5 4   ◇ Q 7 3
♣ A 8 7 6 3   ♣ K 9 4

♠ A 9 6
♡ Q 10 9 6 5 3
◇ J 9 2
♣ J

South opened a Weak 2♡ Bid and North raised to 4♡, not sure who could make what. West led the ♠J to dummy's ♠K.

Declarer led dummy's ♣2 to his ♣J and West's ♣A. West shifted to the ◇6, but declarer won dummy's ◇K and led dummy's ♣Q.

East covered, but duck or cover he was toast. Declarer ruffed his ♣K and later discarded a diamond loser on dummy's ♣10.

How should East and West have defended?

South's Weak 2♡ Bid likely was not based on *two* outside aces. So West was marked with the ♣A as soon as East was able to place South with the ♠A at Trick 1. Thus it was routine for East to win the ♣K at Trick 2 to avoid being caught in a ruffing finesse position with his king later.

Careful defense leaves declarer with four losers: a club, a diamond and two hearts. Down one.

DEAL 54. ANOTHER RUFFING FINESSE PROBLEM

                         ♠ Q 10 2
                         ♡ Q J 8 3 2
                         ◊ A 9 4
                         ♣ A Q
        ♠ 8 5   ♠ 9
        ♡ A 9 7 6   ♡ K 5 4
        ◊ 10 8 5 2   ◊ K Q J
        ♣ 10 7 2   ♣ K J 9 8 6 4
                         ♠ A K J 7 6 4 3
                         ♡ 10
                         ◊ 7 6 3
                         ♣ 5 3

After East overcalled North's 1♡ opening with 2♣, South's 4♠ ended the auction. South won Trick 1 with dummy's ♣A and led the ♡2 to Trick 2.

West captured South's ♡10 and continued clubs. Upon winning the ♣K, East shifted to the ◊K, driving out dummy's ◊A.

East covered dummy's ♡Q with the ♡K, but South ruffed. Then South cashed the ♠A. crossed to dummy's ♠10 and ruffed a low heart high. South reentered dummy with the ♠Q and discarded two diamonds on dummy's high ♡J8. Making five spades.

Could East expect to defeat the contract if declarer had the ♡A?

In the other room, East didn't think so. He rose with the ♡K when declarer led the ♡2 from dummy. East cashed the ♣K and led the ◊K.

After winning dummy's ◊A, declarer tried the same ruffing finesse against the outstanding ♡A, but here it failed. West, not East, had the heart honor against which South tried the ruffing finesse.

Declarer lost one heart, two diamonds, and one club. Down one.

DEAL 55. THE MAGIC OF SPOT CARDS

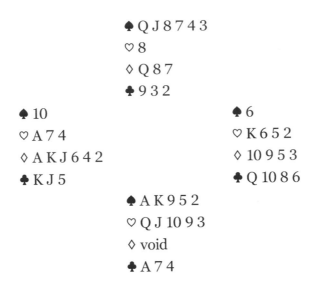

♠ Q J 8 7 4 3
♡ 8
♢ Q 8 7
♣ 9 3 2

♠ 10
♡ A 7 4
♢ A K J 6 4 2
♣ K J 5

♠ 6
♡ K 6 5 2
♢ 10 9 5 3
♣ Q 10 8 6

♠ A K 9 5 2
♡ Q J 10 9 3
♢ void
♣ A 7 4

South, dealer, vul versus non-vul opponents, opened 1♠. West overcalled 2♢. How many spades would you bid with North's hand? North bid 4♠. When East bid 5♢ to save, South bid 6♠. Would you?

West thought briefly of doubling but refrained. He led the ♢K. Declarer ruffed, drew the outstanding trumps with dummy's ♠J and led dummy's ♡8 to West's ♡A. West shifted alertly to the ♣5.

South captured East's ♣Q with the ♣A, then crossruffed. Heart ruff, diamond ruff, heart ruff, diamond ruff, and a third heart ruff in dummy to set up his fifth heart. He could still reach his hand with the ♠A and throw one club from dummy on his ♡Q. But he still had to lose a club trick. Down one.

Could declarer have made 6♠?

Perhaps. After the same wild auction in the other room, West doubled 6♠. South ruffed the ♢K opening lead and led the ♡3 from his hand immediately.

Would you have played the ♡A on air at Trick 2? West didn't. East won the ♡K and shifted to the ♣10. South won the ♣A. He drew the trumps and took a ruffing heart finesse against West. He was able to discard all his club losers and claim his doubled slam.

WHEN

TO

COVER:

TIMING

DEAL 56. SECOND HAND HIGH: COVER AN HONOR?

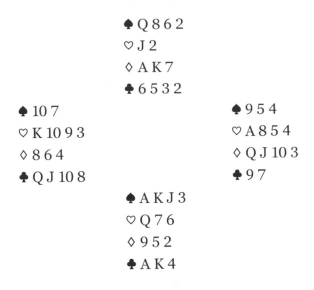

♠ Q 8 6 2
♡ J 2
◊ A K 7
♣ 6 5 3 2

♠ 10 7
♡ K 10 9 3
◊ 8 6 4
♣ Q J 10 8

♠ 9 5 4
♡ A 8 5 4
◊ Q J 10 3
♣ 9 7

♠ A K J 3
♡ Q 7 6
◊ 9 5 2
♣ A K 4

South reached 4♠ via a Stayman auction. He visualized four likely losers: two hearts and one in each minor, when West led the ♣Q.

It seemed unlikely that clubs would split 3-3, and more unlikely still that West would have both top hearts. South won the ♣A and crossed to dummy's ♠Q to start hearts with dummy's ♡J. East played low West won the ♡K. West's ♣10 continuation drove out declarer's ♣K.

South drew only one more round of trumps before entering dummy with the ◊K to led dummy's last heart. East rose with the ♡A and drove out dummy's ◊A with the ◊Q. Declarer returned to his hand with the ♠K and discarded dummy's diamond loser on the established ♡Q.

How could the defenders have worked out the killing defense?

South in the other room adopted the same line. But East thought to get some bang for his buck: a jack, not a deuce, with his ace. He captured the ♡J with his ♡A. If South had ♡K10x, no defense could keep him from scoring a heart trick anyway.

The only losing case for playing the ace was if South had a doubleton ♡K10 precisely. A risk worth taking! Now declarer was helpless to make the contract, having no place to park a minor-suit loser.

DEAL 57. THE CHAMBERMAID'S SON'S RULE

```
                    ♠ 8 6 5
                    ♡ 4
                    ◊ A K Q 10 4 3
    Joe             ♣ 7 6 2          Post-Mortimer
    ♠ J                              ♠ K Q 9 7 3
    ♡ Q J 10                         ♡ 8 7 6 5 3 2
    ◊ J 9 8 7 5                      ◊ void
    ♣ K J 9 4                        ♣ Q 5
                    ♠ A 10 4 2
                    ♡ A K 9
                    ◊ 6 2
                    ♣ A 10 8 3
```

In the fancy North-South methods, North transferred to diamonds after South opened 1NT, then showed a singleton or void in hearts. South became declarer in 3NT on an different auction. As Fred Hamilton once said about similar methods, "What? And tell them what to lead against three notrump?" West had a normal ♡Q opening lead regardless.

Needing only five tricks from diamonds, South, Safety-First Sophie, won the ♡A and led the ◊6 to Trick 2. She let it ride when West followed with the ◊5. East, Post-Mortimer Snide, was livid when Sophie repeated the diamond finesse and wound up with 10 tricks.

"That's one more IMP you owe me, Joe. The Chambermaid's Son's Rule says, 'When you have an opponent's card surrounded, play the top sheet, not the bottom,'" ranted Mort. "I'll have to teach that to my teammates," said Sophie. "One of them is a chambermaid's daughter."

"Rose? No wonder she wears second-hand clothes!" sneered Mort.

How did an expert South take only eight tricks in the other room?

Reaching 3NT via another route, he won the ♡A and thought to safety-play diamonds by taking a first-round finesse against the ◊J. However, when Rose played the ◊J at Trick 2, he had it surrounded. He played dummy's ◊Q. Curtains---er, sheets!

DEAL 58. SECOND HAND HIGH: DUCK OR COVER?

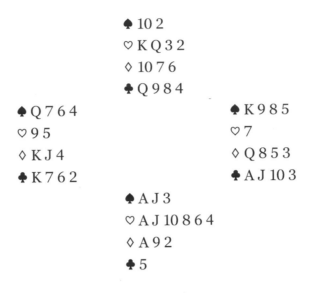

♠ 10 2
♡ K Q 3 2
♢ 10 7 6
♣ Q 9 8 4

♠ Q 7 6 4
♡ 9 5
♢ K J 4
♣ K 7 6 2

♠ K 9 8 5
♡ 7
♢ Q 8 5 3
♣ A J 10 3

♠ A J 3
♡ A J 10 8 6 4
♢ A 9 2
♣ 5

South opened 1♡ and North raised to 2♡, but aggressive competition by East and West pushed North-South to a precarious 4♡.

Fearing to blow a trick by leading any other suit, West led the ♡5. Declarer won in dummy to float the ♠10. East ducked and West's ♠Q won.

Declarer won West's trump exit in dummy and hooked the ♠J. That was a "free" finesse, as the ♠A would provide a useful discard from dummy even if the ♠J lost to the ♠K, but of course South placed East with a spade honor for his double of 2♡.

South lost only three tricks: one in each suit but trumps. Making 4♡.

Could the defenders have taken a fourth trick?

Yes, on a diamond lead, or a club lead and a diamond shift, but that was not the only way.

In the other room, West also led a passive trump, but when South led the ♠10 from dummy at Trick 2, East reasoned, "If the king must die in battle, let him take an enemy soldier with him." So he covered.

Declarer beheaded East's ♠K with the ♠A, but had no place to park one of dummy's diamond losers. A second diamond loser meant down one.

DEAL 59. SECOND HAND HIGH TO
CONTINUE THE DEFENSE

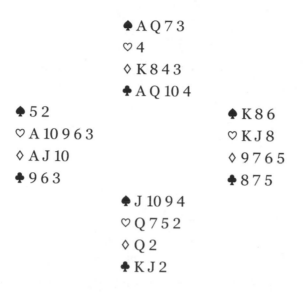

♠ A Q 7 3
♡ 4
◇ K 8 4 3
♣ A Q 10 4

♠ 5 2
♡ A 10 9 6 3
◇ A J 10
♣ 9 6 3

♠ K 8 6
♡ K J 8
◇ 9 7 6 5
♣ 8 7 5

♠ J 10 9 4
♡ Q 7 5 2
◇ Q 2
♣ K J 2

Lighter and lighter grow the "third seat" openings. Neither West's 1♡ nor East's 2♡ raise over North's takeout double shut out South's spades. North was charmed to raise 2♠ to 4♠.

Envisioning multiple heart ruffs in dummy, West led the ♠2. Declarer played low from dummy. East won the ♠K and continued the ♠6. South won dummy's ♠Q to start hearts from dummy. West captured South's ♡Q with the ♡A and exited in clubs. Declarer won in hand, ruffed a heart in dummy and led to the ◇Q.

West won the ◇A to continue clubs, but declarer won in hand again and managed the rest. He ruffed another heart with dummy's ♠A, and discarded his last heart on dummy's fourth club. Making 4♡.

Could the defenders have defeated 4♡?

In the other room, the play began similarly, but perceiving a need to draw trumps, East hopped up with the ♡K and led his last trump. The defense had one more hurdle to surmount. When declarer led the 2◇ through him, West had to duck.

West was up to the task. Dummy's ◇K won and declarer threw his ◇Q on dummy's fourth club, but that yielded only nine tricks: four clubs, one diamond, two spades and one ruff in each hand.

DEAL 60. SHOULD SHE GET A NEW BOYFRIEND?

```
                       ♠ A 6 4 3
                       ♡ J 7 3
                       ◇ J 2
        Bambi          ♣ A J 4 3        Steve
        ♠ 9 8 7                         ♠ Q J 10 2
        ♡ A Q 6                         ♡ 5 4
        ◇ 10 8 7 4                      ◇ A 9 6
        ♣ 9 6 5                         ♣ Q 10 8 7
                       ♠ K 5
        Danny          ♡ K 10 9 8 2
                       ◇ K Q 5 3
                       ♣ K 2
```

Bambi, Danny's kibitzee, led a safe ♠9 against South's 4♡. Declarer won in dummy to start diamonds with the ◇J. When it held declarer led dummy's last diamond.

"Fool me once, shame on you, fool me twice, shame on me!" said East as he played his ◇A. He shifted to the ♡5. Bambi won two hearts and exited with her third heart, but that was all for the defense. Making 4♡.

This was the last board of the match. Danny followed Bambi into the Closed Room, where play had already finished. Bambi's boyfriend was livid when he learned that Moshe in the Closed Room, had gone down two.

"You lost a *club* trick besides going down?" he said to Moshe.

How did that happen?

Moshe explained when he won dummy's ♠A at Trick 1 to start diamonds with dummy's ◇J. Arthur Acecasher, East won the ◇A and shifted to the ♡4. West cleared the suit. Needing a diamond discard, Moshe finessed dummy's ♣J.

Moshe said, "Sorry, Steve, I should have held it to down one. I owe you an IMP." "That makes three IMPs you owe just from tonight," growled Steve. Bambi whispered in Danny's ear, "Shall I get a new boyfriend?"

Danny blushed and said, "What took you so long to ask?"

DEAL 61. SECOND HAND HIGH FOR BETTER TIMING

```
                    ♠ K 10 9 6 3
                    ♡ K 5 3 2
                    ◊ Q J
                    ♣ 8 3
    ♠ 5 2                           ♠ 7
    ♡ Q J 6 4                       ♡ A 10 9 8
    ◊ K 9 3 2                       ◊ 8 7 5 4
    ♣ A 10 5                        ♣ K 9 7 2
                    ♠ A Q J 8 4
                    ♡ 7
                    ◊ A 10 6
                    ♣ Q J 6 4
```

"Never pass a 4-trump limit raise with a singleton!" Jim heard it from his teacher, the late great Bernie Chazen, who was very right in emphasizing the large difference between three and four-card support.

How's that for a "rule"? We'd all go on to 4♠ with the South hand even if it contained the ◊K instead of the ◊A, and we'd have four losers off the top. Jim says North's jump to 3♠ was marginal.

Things looked bleak when West led the ♡Q against 4♠. South ducked the ♡Q and ruffed when West continued the ♡J. He crossed to dummy's ♠9 and led the ♣3 to his ♣Q. West won the ♣A and tapped declarer with a third heart.

South drew the last trump with dummy's ♠K and led dummy's last club. East won the ♣K and shifted to diamonds. South rose with the ◊A, threw dummy's last diamond on the ♣J and crossruffed the rest. Making 4♠.

Could a stronger defense have defeated 4♠?

In the other room, Rose, East, appreciated the need to lead up to West's hoped-for ◊K early. As West was unlikely to have both top diamonds or the ♠A, a successful defense required two club tricks, so she placed West with the ♣A. Time was of the essence!

Rose put up the ♣K at Trick 4 to shoot the ◊8 through. Declarer was through. No way to avoid two losers in the red suits and two top clubs.

DEAL 62. SECOND HAND HIGH FOR TIMING

$\spadesuit$ K 10 3 2
$\heartsuit$ 10 2
$\diamond$ A K 10 6 5
$\clubsuit$ Q 3

$\spadesuit$ A 6
$\heartsuit$ A 9 7 5
$\diamond$ Q 9 7 2
$\clubsuit$ K 10 7

$\spadesuit$ 5 4
$\heartsuit$ K 8 6 4
$\diamond$ J 8
$\clubsuit$ 9 8 6 5 2

$\spadesuit$ Q J 9 8 7
$\heartsuit$ Q J 3
$\diamond$ 4 3
$\clubsuit$ A J 4

West did well to stay silent when North opened 1$\diamond$ behind him and South responded 1$\spadesuit$. When his opponents crept up to 4$\spadesuit$, West placed his partner with at best meager strength, so he went passive by leading the $\spadesuit$A and another.

Declarer won dummy's $\spadesuit$K and led the $\heartsuit$2 to his $\heartsuit$Q. West won and seeing no safe exit elsewhere, he returned the $\heartsuit$5 to East's $\heartsuit$K. Now declarer's $\heartsuit$J provided a discard for dummy's $\clubsuit$3. Making four spades.

Declarer had three top tricks in the minors and a crossruff for the rest.

How could the defenders have done better?

With better timing. Had East stepped up with his $\heartsuit$K on the first heart play to lead the $\clubsuit$9 through, West could have taken the setting trick with the $\clubsuit$K before declarer could set up the $\heartsuit$J to discard a club from dummy.

DEAL 63. TIMING: SECOND HAND HIGH

                           ♠ K J 9 3
                           ♡ J 10 7 5
                           ◊ A 8 6 3
                           ♣ 5

    ♠ 4   ♠ 7 6
    ♡ A 8 6 3   ♡ K 9 2
    ◊ K Q 10   ◊ 9 4 2
    ♣ Q J 10 6 3   ♣ K 9 7 4 2

                           ♠ A Q 10 8 5 2
                           ♡ Q 4
                           ◊ J 7 5
                           ♣ A 8

North's "Jordan" 2NT response over West's double of 1♠ depicted a limit raise or better, but enabled East to bid a lead-suggesting 3♣. That made little difference as West had a normal ♣Q opening lead against the eventual 4♠ anyway.

South won the ♣A and drew trumps with the ♠A and ♠K before starting hearts with dummy's ♡5. West captured declarer's ♡Q with the ♡A and shifted to the ◊K. Declarer played low from dummy and East played a discouraging ◊2.

West could do no better than continue clubs. Declarer ruffed in dummy and tried to slip dummy's ♡10 through. East rose with the ♡K to return the ◊9, driving out dummy's ◊A. Too late! South threw his ◊J on North's ♡J and had only trumps left. Making 4♠.

"Where were you when I needed you?" asked West.

West was guilty of lese majeste. for he was addressing the ♡K.

In the other room, His Majesty joined the battle early. An alert East hurled him into the fray on the first heart lead from dummy. Then he shifted to the ◊9 through declarer *before* dummy's ♡J became established.

DEAL 64. WHAT KIND OF SOUP DID HE HAVE?

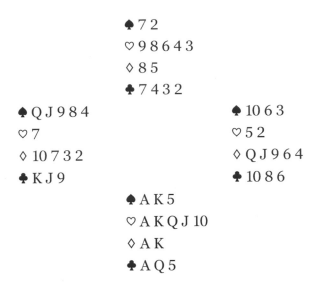

```
                  ♠ 7 2
                  ♡ 9 8 6 4 3
                  ◇ 8 5
                  ♣ 7 4 3 2
   ♠ Q J 9 8 4                  ♠ 10 6 3
   ♡ 7                          ♡ 5 2
   ◇ 10 7 3 2                   ◇ Q J 9 6 4
   ♣ K J 9                      ♣ 10 8 6
                  ♠ A K 5
                  ♡ A K Q J 10
                  ◇ A K
                  ♣ A Q 5
```

South opened an Omnibus 2♣, rebid a "Kokish" 2♡ to show hearts or a balanced game-forcing hand over North's neutral 2◇ response, and bid a leisurely 2NT next. North bid 3◇, a Jacoby Transfer to show hearts.

South replied with a super-duper-whooper (is this a big enough word for it?) acceptance of 6♡. North was unable to retreat therefrom.

Declarer won the opening spade lead, drew trumps, and stripped the diamonds and spades. After ruffing his last spade in dummy, he tackled clubs by leading dummy's ♣7.

East reached for the ♣6 to show count, but stopped in mid-motion. He eyed South suspiciously and covered with the ♣8. Hmmm, thought South. If the ♣K is on side, it will still be on side on the next turn. So he ducked. West won the ♣9 and was endplayed.

"Ruff-sluff or come to Papa," said South, showing his hand. 6♡ made.
"I could have used a little help from you, pard," said West. "Who, me?" answered East. "I had borscht."
Just what kind of soup did he have?

Chicken noodle soup, good for whatever ails you. East's ♣10 was the cure for all ills. Had he played it, West could have underplayed the ♣9.

Of course, if South had the ♣9, he'd have had a perfect elimination, being able to cover any club that East might play and claim the slam.

DEAL 65. DUCK OR COVER?

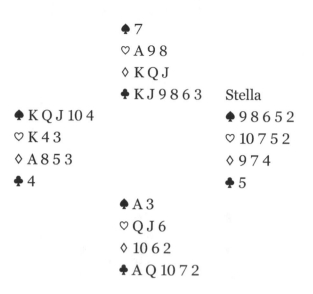

```
                    ♠ 7
                    ♡ A 9 8
                    ◇ K Q J
                    ♣ K J 9 8 6 3    Stella
    ♠ K Q J 10 4                     ♠ 9 8 6 5 2
    ♡ K 4 3                          ♡ 10 7 5 2
    ◇ A 8 5 3                        ◇ 9 7 4
    ♣ 4                              ♣ 5
                    ♠ A 3
                    ♡ Q J 6
                    ◇ 10 6 2
                    ♣ A Q 10 7 2
```

Look at the North hand. What would you respond to South's 1♣ opening using standard methods? You might respond 1◇ or a 2◇ jump shift to show a forcing club raise. Playing inverted minors of course would make this hand no problem. But West overcalled 1♠ and North gambled 6♣.

South might have had (a) ♠KQ3 ♡K63 ◇A43 ♣Q1072 (off two aces) or (b) ♠A86 ♡10763 ◇A9 ♣AQ73 (off two heart tricks) or worse.

Fortunately, he didn't. He won the spade lead, drew trump with the ♣A, led the ♡Q and captured West's ♡K with dummy's ♡A. Then a successful finesse against East's ♡10 brought 6♣ home.

"Lucky, lucky," said East, Stella by Starlight. Was Stella right?

Lucky also that West rushed to cover the first heart. In the other room North saw West's 1♠ and bid 4NT, hoping South would interpret it as Roman Keycard Blackwood and *not* have a hand like (a) or (b).

Lucky on both counts, but unlucky to have an able defender sitting West. This West waited to cover South's *second* heart honor. Later, East's ♡10 took the setting trick. Against normal defense, 6♣ was doomed.

IT'S A
SINGLETON:
WIN OR DUCK?

SECOND HAND HIGH? NOT SO FAST!

So far we have examined many deals in which a defender, for one reason or another, must rise to the occasion by playing high as second to play to a trick. These deals illustrate *exceptions*.

They are not, however, the exceptions that most bridge players make. Now let's look at those exceptions---exceptions that should *not* be made. Here is the most common:

North (dummy) 9

East (you) A 7 5 2

Should you play your ace on air when declarer leads dummy's singleton?

Drumroll, please: "Yes, no and maybe!"

Yes, if this will be the setting trick; you should probably take it.

Otherwise, probably no, though of course we should see the other suits, the auction, and the play to the previous tricks to be confident.

Let's see why. Suppose this is the layout:

$$9$$

Q 10 6 4 3   A 7 5 2

$$K J 8$$

If you play low, declarer must guess. He may play the jack, thinking you would always play the ace if you had it. This assumes that you duck smoothly.

So don't take our caption "Not So Fast!" literally. Play your card in *your normal tempo*.

For some players, that is fast, but regardless, avoid fumbling over whether to follow with the seven or the five. If you really find that a problem, solve it early, before the current trick.

Here is another position:

                           3
     J 10 6 4   A 9 7 2
                         K Q 8 5

We have seen this position when declarer leads a singleton from his hand towards honors in dummy:

                    (dummy) K Q 8 5
       (you) A 7 5 2

Well, not exactly. Here you may not know that declarer's three is a singleton. Declarer might be leading low from a doubleton or tripleton jack, for example, and you may have to wait to capture his jack with your ace. Here ducking often sacrifices one fast trick to get two slow tricks.

This is the same from the other side of the looking glass.

Here's another layout:

                           3
     K 8 6 2   A 9 7 5
                        Q J 10 4

In a suit contract, declarer may be planning a ruffing finesse.

Remember our discussing who should win the first trick for the defense? Yes, the defender whose honor lies in front of, not behind, the hand with the sequence of honors.

Here that is West. So as East, you must let partner win his king, *the honor that can be ruff-finessed,* first.

Have you noticed that *except* for the setting trick, ducking is almost always right. Yet what do we usually see at the table? Yes, ace-risers.

Danny is in a race with Eddie Kantar for the dubious honor in the Guinness Book of World Records: *Most Aces Lost by Ducking, Lifetime,* which he says will make a good companion for the other record he claims (*Most tricks lost to Singleton Kings on Side*).

DEAL 66. THE OPPOSITE: SECOND HAND HIGH? NO, LOW

```
                        ♠ 7
                        ♡ K Q J 8 6 3
                        ◇ K 6 2
                        ♣ A 5 2
        ♠ J 9 6 3 2                      ♠ A 10 8 5
        ♡ 7                              ♡ 4
        ◇ Q J 10 9                       ◇ 8 5 4 3
        ♣ K 8 4                          ♣ Q J 10 9
                        ♠ K Q 4
                        ♡ A 10 9 5 2
                        ◇ A 7
                        ♣ 7 6 3
```

South opened 1♡ and North bid 4NT. South puzzled whether North meant it as Old-Fashioned or Roman Keycard Blackwood, but realized that his reply was 5♡ either way. Disappointed that an ace was missing, North bid only 6♡.

Declarer captured West's ◇Q opening lead with dummy's ◇K, and to avoid giving either defender a chance to signal in some other suit, led the ♠7 from dummy. "No overtricks for you!" said East as he rose with the ♠A.

South won the diamond return with his ◇A, drew trumps with the ♡9, threw two clubs from dummy on his spade monarchs, and claimed.

How did the defenders beat 6♡ in the other room?

The auction differed, as North splintered with 3♠ initially. South rebid 3NT, and North bid Kickback 4♠, a Roman Keycard ask.

Although a daring club lead would have yielded down two, West led a stodgy ◇Q. However, when declarer led dummy's singleton spade, East played the ♠8.

East never won his ♠A, but the defenders earned two club tricks in exchange. Down one. Courage!

DEAL 67. SECOND HAND HIGH? BETTER GO LOW

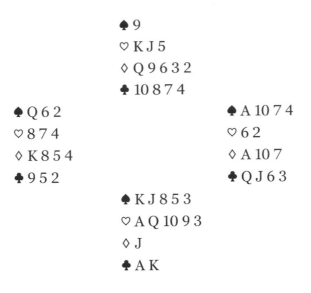

After opening 1♠ as dealer and receiving a 1NT response, South forced to game with a 3♡ jump shift and rebid 4♡ over North's 3NT. Fearing spade ruffs in dummy, West led the ♡4.

Declarer won dummy's ♡J to lead the ♠9.

"Nobody steals any tricks against me when I have the ace," said East as he plunked down the ♠A proudly. Then he returned his last trump to cut down on dummy's ruffing power as his partner had thought to do.

Declarer won in hand, ruffed a spade in dummy, returned to his hand in clubs to draw the last trump. East's two aces were the only tricks for the defense. Making four hearts with an overtrick.

How did the declarer in the other room fail even to make four?

After receiving the same good opening lead, the other South also led dummy's ♠9. There, however, East played low (smoothly please). Declarer finessed the ♠J. West won the ♠Q and continued trumps. South won in hand to ruff a spade with dummy's last trump. But he wound up with only one long spade trick to go with one spade ruff, two top clubs and his five trump tricks; only nine tricks in all.

East didn't lose his ♠A, he *invested* it. He got it back with two tricks interest. Even if South had guessed to play the ♠K at Trick 2, East would have gotten his investment back.

DEAL 68. THE LADY OR THE TIGER?

```
                        ♠ K Q J 4
                        ♡ 9 7 3
                        ◇ A K Q 8 4
                        ♣ 9
        ♠ 8 5                           ♠ 9 7 6
        ♡ Q J 10 6 4                    ♡ K 8 5
        ◇ 9 7                           ◇ 10 6 5 3
        ♣ Q 10 5 2                      ♣ A 8 3
                        ♠ A 10 3 2
                        ♡ A 2
                        ◇ J 2
                        ♣ K J 7 6 4
```

Once South rebid 1♠, North used some fancy footwork to propel the pair to 6♠. West led the ♡Q. South won the ♡A, drew trumps and ran diamonds, discarding two clubs and the ♡2.

In the four-card ending, declarer led dummy's singleton ♣9. East leapt upon it like a tiger with his ♣A and tried to cash the ♡K. South ruffed, threw a heart from dummy on his ♣K and crossruffed the last two tricks.

Making 6♠.

How did South go down in 6♠ in the other room?

In the other room, the play began the same, but when declarer led dummy's ♣9 to Trick 10, East was ready. He ducked smoothly.

Faced with a guess, South finessed the ♣J. After winning the ♣Q, West continued hearts.

Declarer crossruffed Tricks 11 and 12, but his ♣K was not high and he had no place to park dummy's last heart. Down one.

East's duck could not possibly cost. If South had both club monarchs, 12 tricks were inevitable regardless. East's only chance was to make South guess ... by girding himself early to duck in tempo.

DEAL 69. ONLY A 2-IMP SWING

```
                    ♠ A J 10 7 6
                    ♡ J 10
                    ♦ 5
                    ♣ Q J 7 6 5
    ♠ K 9 3 2                      ♠ Q 8 4
    ♡ 6 3 2                        ♡ 8 4
    ♦ Q 4                          ♦ A 9 6 3 2
    ♣ K 10 8 3                     ♣ 9 4 2
                    ♠ 5
                    ♡ A K Q 9 7 5
                    ♦ K J 10 8 7
                    ♣ A
```

When North rebid 3♡ over South's 3♦ jump shift, South mistook a preference for a raise and tried for slam in the only way he knew: Blackwood! On learning that an ace was missing, he signed off with 5♡.

West led the ♣3, the unbid suit. Declarer won the ♣A and crossed to dummy's ♠A to start diamonds from dummy.

"Oh no!" said East, who fancied himself an expert. He rose with the ♦A, eager to continue clubs. Declarer ruffed and ruffed a diamond in dummy. Upon seeing West's ♦Q fall, South drew the remaining trumps and took the rest to make an overtrick. Plus 480.

East lectured South, "Don't you know that when there's only one ace missing, you *must* bid slam? Our teammates will reach six hearts easily."

Was East right?

Right about a Blackwood asker's commitment to slam when only one key card is missing. Wrong about everything else. In the other room, South stopped sensibly in 4♡. West led a trump and South started diamonds from dummy at Trick 1. East played the ♦2 in tempo, and West captured South's ♦J with the ♦Q.

The trump continuation removed dummy's last trump, and South lost two more tricks. Plus 420. The East who grabbed the ♦A took one diamond trick. The East who ducked managed three diamond tricks.

Arriving to compare scores at the end of the match, East in the Open Room asked his teammate South, "Did you bid six hearts on Board 8?"

"Thankfully, no," answered South. "Losing only two IMPs."

DEAL 70. ONLY A 2-IMP SWING?

```
                      ♠ 8
                      ♡ Q J 5 4 3
                      ◊ Q 8 7 5
                      ♣ Q 8 6
       ♠ 10 3                        ♠ A J 7 4 2
       ♡ 9 7                         ♡ A 6
       ◊ A J 10 6 4                  ◊ K 2
       ♣ J 7 5 3                     ♣ K 9 4 2
                      ♠ K Q 9 6 5
                      ♡ K 10 8 2
                      ◊ 9 3
                      ♣ A 10
```

South opened 1♠ and North responded 1NT. He passed South's 2♡ rebid. West made the normal lead of a trump. East won the ♡A and returned a trump to dummy's ♡J.

Declarer led dummy's spade, but East rose promptly with the ♠A. West dropped the ♠10 in a valiant effort to show suit-preference for diamonds. East switched bravely to the ◊K. When it held, he continued with the ◊2 to West's ◊A. "Whew!" exclaimed East. "Got all our tricks!"

Was he right?

Yes, in the sense the defenders had taken the last of their tricks. Declarer had two spades, one club, one diamond, and five trumps by crossruffing coming: one trick to burn. North-South +140.

No, a fifth trick was available. In the other room, North raised to 3♡. The play began the same, but East ducked when declarer led dummy's ♠8 to Trick 3. South won the ♠Q for his second trick. Five tricks crossruffing and the ♣A brought the total only to eight. North-South -100.

"Take the first spade and we'll beat them another," said West.

"Two IMPs more."

"Sorry," said East, not wanting to antagonize a client. But of course playing the ♠A on air would have cost the 6 IMPs he earned by ducking.

DEAL 71. SECOND HAND HIGH? NO, PLAY LOW

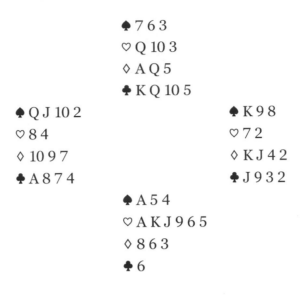

```
                    ♠ 7 6 3
                    ♡ Q 10 3
                    ◇ A Q 5
                    ♣ K Q 10 5
    ♠ Q J 10 2                      ♠ K 9 8
    ♡ 8 4                           ♡ 7 2
    ◇ 10 9 7                        ◇ K J 4 2
    ♣ A 8 7 4                       ♣ J 9 3 2
                    ♠ A 5 4
                    ♡ A K J 9 6 5
                    ◇ 8 6 3
                    ♣ 6
```

West led the ♠Q against 4♡. South won the ♠A and cashed two hearts. Then he led the ♣6. West hopped ♣A and continued spades, but dummy's clubs provided discards for declarer's diamonds and 4♡ rolled home.

How did the defense prevail in the other room?

West simply ducked when South led his singleton club. West's only hope to beat 4♡ was for East to have the ◇K and ◇J behind dummy.

West lost one club trick but gained two diamond tricks in return. With only his six trump tricks and one trick in each other suit, declarer came up a trick short.

Positions like this are commonplace. Without a compelling reason to rise, such as ensuring the defeat of a contract or an urgent need to be on lead, you'll do well to duck a guarded ace when a singleton is led through you. The trick usually comes back, typically with interest.

DEAL 72. YOU BE THE JURY!

```
                    ♠ K Q 7 5 2
                    ♡ K 8
                    ◊ J 7 3
                    ♣ A J 6
        ♠ A 10 8 4                  ♠ J 6 3
        ♡ 6 5 3                     ♡ 10 7
        ◊ 10 9 2                    ◊ A K 6 5
        ♣ Q 9 3                     ♣ K 10 8 4
                    ♠ 9
                    ♡ A Q J 9 4 2
                    ◊ Q 8 4
                    ♣ 7 5 2
```

If you switch from Standard American to Two-Over-One Game Forcing, as the North-South pair here did, you can no longer bid 1♠-2♡; 2♠-3♡ with hands like South's, and 1♠-1NT (forcing); 2♠-3♡ wouldn't do the hand justice. So maybe you'll do well to play 1♠-3♡ as invitational?

Should North then raise to 4♡? He did on this deal. West led the ◊10. East took both top diamonds and led a third, hoping that West had led from ◊Q109 or ◊109.

South won the ◊Q and led the ♠9. West rose with the ♠A and it was all over. Dummy's ♠A won Trick 5. Soon enough, South's two remaining club losers went away on dummy's ♠KQ. Making 4♠.

Could the defenders have done better? You be the jury!

In the other room, the defenders beat 4♡. After the same start, West ducked the spade; South had no place to park *both* club losers. Down one.

In defense of the first West, note that South might have had a different hand, e.g. ♠9 ♡QJ109742 ◊Q84 ♣K5. In that case, East could have saved the day by cashing the ♡A at Trick 3 to tell West to take the setting trick.

Or could he? What if South had ♠A ♡Q1076532 ◊Q84 ♣K5, *two* likely trump losers if left to his own devices? This calls for a hung jury.

So we say, *we don't know.* But ... *when in doubt, duck.*

DEAL 73. WIN OR DUCK?

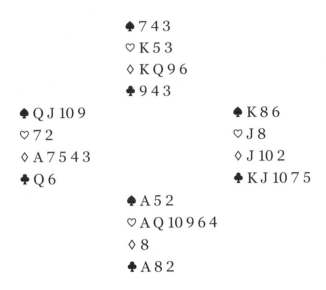

West led the ♠Q against a pushy 4♡. South won the ♠A and led the ◊8. West snatched the ◊A promptly so the defenders could take their two established spade tricks.

Declarer won the club shift, drew trumps with the ♡AQ, led a third trump to dummy's ♡K, and threw two clubs on dummy's diamond monarchs.

Making 4♡.

How did the defense prevail in the other room?

West beat 4♡ simply by withholding his ◊A until the last chance to take it. That chance never came, but for West's one-trick investment in diamonds, the defenders earned two tricks in clubs.

Down one.

DEAL 74. ANOTHER LOW WITH A SINGLETON

                          ♠ K 9 6 5 2
                          ♡ 5
                          ◊ K Q 5 4
                          ♣ 8 5 3

    ♠ 7 3   ♠ 8 4
    ♡ J 10 8 4   ♡ A 9 7 3 2
    ◊ 10 8 3   ◊ A J 9
    ♣ Q J 9 2   ♣ K 10 4

                          ♠ A Q J 10
                          ♡ K Q 6
                          ◊ 7 6 2
                          ♣ A 7 6

North's 2♡ Jacoby Transfer let East make a lead-directing double. That had the paradoxical effect of pushing North and South into a marginal 4♠, as South liked his well-placed ♡KQx and North liked his singleton.

West led a dutiful ♡J. East won the ♡A, but it was "game over" as South won the club shift and drew trumps in two rounds. Then he threw dummy's remaining clubs on the ♡KQ, and lost two diamond tricks when the ◊A sat behind dummy's honors. Making 4♠.

Was it East's fault, for heeding Mother Goose's "Third hand high?"

East's fault, yes, but not for the reason you may think. From his perspective, West might have had ♠xx ♡KJ10x ◊10xx ♣Jxxx, so East couldn't know to duck West's ♡J at Trick 1.

East blew the defense during the auction. With strength scattered among three suits, he had no reason to beg for a lead in any one of them. Indeed. East would have preferred a lead in either of the other two suits.

In the other room, East kept silent. South accepted North's game invitation. West made his most attractive opening lead, the ♣Q and there was no way for East to go wrong later.

When declarer led the ♡5 from dummy later, East did well to play low, following the "duck one to save two" principle, but even playing the ♡A on air would beat 4♠.

DEAL 75. EMERGENCY FLASHERS

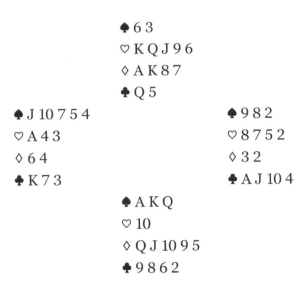

```
              ♠ 6 3
              ♡ K Q J 9 6
              ◊ A K 8 7
              ♣ Q 5
♠ J 10 7 5 4              ♠ 9 8 2
♡ A 4 3                  ♡ 8 7 5 2
◊ 6 4                    ◊ 3 2
♣ K 7 3                  ♣ A J 10 4
              ♠ A K Q
              ♡ 10
              ◊ Q J 10 9 5
              ♣ 9 8 6 2
```

South bid 3NT after North raised his 2◊ to North's 1♥ opening response to 3◊.
West led the ♠5 to East's ♠8 and declarer's ♠K. When South led the ♡10 to Trick 2,
West ducked, thinking to wait for Godot---er,

a second round---to take his ace.

There was no second round. Having two tricks in the bag, declarer ran home with
two more spade tricks and five diamonds, nine in all.

Should West have beaten 3NT? Were there enough clues?

Yes. In the other room, West counted declarer's tricks. When East could play no
spade higher than the ♠8 to Trick 1, South was marked with three top spades, and
the 2◊ response strongly suggested a five-card suit. That makes eight, and even one
heart trick makes nine.

Had South been a passed hand, the killing defense might have been easier for West,
as declarer could hardly have the ♣A too, but it was easy enough anyhow.

Hop with the ♡A, then clubs, taking care to cash the ♣K first to prevent accidents
such as a spade return from East after winning the ♣A, and down declarer goes.

DEAL 76. GRADUATION DAY

♠ A K 7 4 3
♡ K Q 10
◊ K Q
♣ K Q 5

♠ Q J 10 9 6
♡ 8 5 2
◊ A J
♣ A J 7

Several writers are violently against Blackwood But look at North's hand. Perfect, no? North invoked Roman Keycard Blackwood promptly over South's 1♠ opening and stopped in 6♠ upon learning that an ace was missing.

South won West's ◊10 opening lead in dummy, drew trumps with dummy's ♠AK, and stripped both minors before leading the ♡8 from hand. West played the ♡6 and East followed with the ♡7 as dummy's ♡Q won.

Declarer returned to his hand with the ♠Q to lead the ♡5 next, West played the ♡9 and ...

Did declarer get it right?

One declarer guessed right, the other didn't. The ♡J was crucial. If Danny ever invents a convention to ask for jacks, what do you think he'll call it? Try to guess before peeking.*

One writer of bridge books who rejected Blackwood was S.J. Simon, author of *Why You Lose at Bridge*. If you haven't read it, put this book down immediately and read that one.

On page 37, Simon said, "So start ducking with your aces. But do not consider yourself graduated until you have successfully ducked with an ace in such a position as to defeat a small slam contract."

Jackwood

PART II
THIRD HAND
HIGH, LOW, OR
OTHER
NOT
TOO HIGH

THIRD HAND HIGH ? NOT SO FAST

Just as we have seen with "second hand low," "third hand high" is not a rule but *at best* a guideline.

Let's consider some general situations against suits at Trick 1:

When partner leads low and from the auction and cards visible to you, you can read it as fourth highest from length and strength, or possibly low from three with dummy having nothing of value in the suit, play high.

In these examples, spades are trump, partner leads a club and declarer plays low from dummy.

(a)

$$♣7\ 6\ 5$$

♣2   ♣A Q 3.

The one card you must *not* play is the ♣3. If you play the ♣3, declarer might win with the ♣8, or underplay the ♣4 and find a miraculous entry to dummy. Your choice is between the ♣A and the ♣Q.

Depending on the auction and what you see in the other suits, you might play either. Before deciding, you must ask yourself, "From what holdings might partner be leading, and why did he lead clubs?"

You can eliminate some holdings. Even though you play "fourth highest from length and strength," partner can hold neither ♣J1082 (else he'd have led the ♣J, top of a broken sequence) nor ♣K1092 (else he'd have led the ♣10, top of an internal sequence). But he might hold ♣J942 or ♣K1082.

Then you must ask yourself, "Is it important not to let declarer win this trick?" It is often important to win Trick 1. If you let declarer win it, he may be able to cash winners in a side suit to discard his own or dummy's club losers.

If it's not important, you must ask yourself what you will do next after winning this trick. Sometimes you won't know. If partner's lead is from ♣10842, for example, winning the ♣A and continuing clubs may let declarer finesse the ♣J successfully without having to use an entry to reach dummy.

So you may be better off playing the ♣Q. Then you'll see whether partner has led from the ♣K (your ♣Q will win) or a lower honor (declarer will win the ♣K, which may guide you to a good shift when you get in later.

If you suspect that declarer has the ♣K, you must consider who will be the first defender to obtain the lead in some other suit. If that's you, you can usually play the ♣Q safely, but if it's partner, win the ♣A to keep him from shifting dangerously to some other suit.

(b)

♣7 6 5

♣2   ♣K Q 8 3

Play the ♣Q. The "rule" is for third hand to play the lowest card that will do the job a hand. Here that job is to prevent declarer from winning a cheap trick with the ♣10 or ♣J. However, there are circumstances in which you should play the ♣K instead. Here are two:

(1) You may expect partner to get in with a trump trick early and want desperately for him to shift to some other suit. To induce him to shift, you must fool him into thinking declarer started with ♣AQ10. Playing the ♣K at Trick 1 will do that job!

(2) You may suspect that partner has ♣1042 and declarer has ♣AJ9. If you expect to get in before partner does, you can hope for two club tricks by inducing declarer to finesse the ♣9 when you return the ♣3. Inconsistency is important here. You must sometimes play the ♣Q and sometimes play the ♣K to give declarer a guess. If *always* play the ♣Q from this holding, an observant opponent will know to play you for the ♣10 when you play the ♣K and return the ♣3 upon obtaining the lead. *Always* playing the ♣K is just as bad.

(c)

♣7 6 5

♣2   ♣Q J 10 4

Play the ♣10. "Lowest card that will do the job" applies. *Unless* you have a very good reason to deceive partner, or partner will not be involved in the defense and you want to deceive declarer. Careful!

(d)

♣Q 6 3

♣2   ♣K 10 4

If declarer plays the ♣3 from dummy, play the ♣10, not the ♣K. Why? Because you have asked yourself "From what holdings might partner's lead be?" "What is my job?" and "What is the lowest card that will do the job?"

Here partner may have led from ♣J972 and you have two jobs. One job is to drive out declarer's ♣A, the other (usually more important) job is to keep dummy's ♣Q from scoring. The ♣10 accomplishes both.

Furthermore, by playing the ♣10, you preserve a *finessing position* against dummy's ♣Q. When partner gets in again, he can pickle dummy's ♣Q by leading the ♣J through.

Or partner may have led from ♣J852. Now there is no finessing position and he can't pickle dummy's ♣Q. But the good news is that he probably won't try, as he knows that *if* you had ♣K1094, you'd have played a "lowest card that will do the job" ♣9, not the ♣10.

(e)

♣J 6 3

♣2   ♣K 9 4

If declarer plays the ♣3 from dummy, play the ♣9, not the ♣K. Why?

Here partner may have led from ♣Q1072. Again you have two jobs, to dislodge declarer's ♣A and (usually more important) to keep dummy's ♣J from scoring. The ♣9 will do both if partner has ♣Q1072, but even if partner has ♣Q872, the ♣9 will do one job.

(f)

♣Q 6 3

♣2   ♣A J 8 4

Here it is clear to play the ♣J. If partner has led from the ♣K, this is the only way to keep dummy's ♣Q from becoming a winner. If partner's only honor is the ♣10, the same is true: you can't keep declarer's ♣K from scoring, so don't even try, but you can keep dummy's ♣Q from scoring and you must play the ♣J to do so.

But hold your horses! If partner has led from ♣10752 *and declarer has a discard coming from dummy*, the ♣A *may be right*. That is why you must seek a panoramic view. Might declarer have ♣K9 and a discard coming from a red-suit winner in dummy, or two discards for dummy's clubs on two red-suit winners in hand?

How many tricks do you need to beat the contract? How many tricks can partner contribute to the defense? How likely is partner to have no better lead than the ♣2 from ♣10752?

You must ponder these questions yourself. We cannot tell you without seeing your other suits, dummy's other suits, and the auction.

Nor can you know what to do without knowing your partner's tendencies. When the auction and his hand do not make the right lead clear: is your partner more likely to seek safety in a passive lead from weakness, or more likely to attack with an aggressive lead from strength?

That being said, when you do not have a panoramic view, we favor ducking as the default

(g)

$$♣Q 6 3$$

$$♣2 \qquad\qquad\qquad ♣A 10 8 4$$

We don't know! If partner has led from ♣J752 or ♣KJ2, you must play the ♣10, but if he has led from ♣K972, you'll look very stupid when declarer captures your ♣10 with his short ♣J.

The lower your second highest card in the suit, the riskier it is to duck. Much as we love to duck, we must draw the line somewhere. This may be where. If not here, then surely when your second highest card is the nine.

(h)

$$♣J 6 3$$

$$♣2 \qquad\qquad\qquad ♣A 10 8 4$$

Here dummy has the jack. Now it is definitely right to play your ace. If you think about it, you'll see why: partner's lead is from ♣Kxxx, ♣Kxx, ♣Qxxx or ♣Qxx, and partner will be able to keep dummy's ♣J from scoring.

(i)

$$♣K 6 4$$

$$♣8 \qquad\qquad\qquad ♣J 5 3 2$$

If partner's ♣8 is a singleton or top of a doubleton, you may think your play doesn't matter as your ♣J is dead in the water regardless. But can you really be confident of partner's club holding?

We think not. Partner's ♣8 might be from ♣Q108 or ♣Q98, in which case you must play the ♣J, the only club high enough to keep declarer from scoring a ♣9 or ♣10 and drive out declarer's ♣A.

100

However, even if you know that partner's ♣8 is singleton or top of a doubleton, the ♣J is still right.

Why? Because your partner is struggling to work out declarer's hand. If you don't play the ♣J, he will think declarer has it. Suppose declarer opened 1NT and reached 4♠ via Stayman or a transfer bid.

Your partner may be counting declarer's "points" and yours. Knowing that you have the ♣J may help him, while thinking that declarer has the ♣J may harm him.

Remember that when you play a card, your partner (we hope) will be asking himself, "From what holdings might you play this card?" and "Why did you play it?" He will answer these questions for himself. Therefore, before you play it, you should ask yourself:

"What will partner think?" and "What would I like partner to think?"

We could go on and on discussing *Suit Combinations for Defenders*. The *Official Encyclopedia of Bridge* (a very useful reference book, but get a 20th-century edition, not the latest one, which is too large to fit in your bookshelf) lists 676 suit combinations *for declarers* showing dummy's holding and declarer's holding in a suit that the defenders *don't* lead and advising declarer how to play the suit if he must start it.

For those 676, the *Encyclopedia* shows the probabilities of success. 676 is a wonderful number, as it's the square of the number of cards held by declarer and dummy, but it only scratches the surface.

Some years ago, Danny calculated just how many suit combinations for declarers there are. Including the "null combination," *void opposite void*, there are 1,594,323. However, there are more suit combinations still for defenders. Given any opening lead, there are 6,908,733 combinations of holdings for dummy and third hand in the suit led.

If you think that in his dotage Danny may have miscounted, please tell us the combinations you think he missed.

We won't show a large number of suit combinations for defenders. Just remember the drill:

"From what holdings might this lead be?"

"What is my job here?"

"Which is the lowest card that will do the job?"

PLEASE DON'T THROW ME UNDER THE BUS

We have all heard the slogan "third hand high" on defense. Why? Either to win the current trick, or to promote a card in your own or your partner's hand for a later trick, *a sacrifice for the greater good.*

How do you promote tricks? By keeping declarer from winning tricks cheaply, which usually means forcing him to expend his sure winners to take them. That's the kernel of truth in "third hand high," not:

"Get rid of your high cards early so you don't have to figure out what to do with them later and can spend your time daydreaming about the aces you'll get next deal."

For example:

♠ 6 3 2

♠7   ♠ K 10 8 4

If spades is an unbid suit, you can almost pinpoint partner's exact holding. He is very unlikely to be leading a singleton or doubleton, so he has ♠J97 or (more likely, as leads from jacks are unattractive) ♠Q97.

The relevant holding for declarer, where your play matters, is ♠AJ5.

You must play the ♠K because any other card will let declarer win a *preventable* trick with his ♠J, and by sacrificing himself the ♠K *promotes* a trick for the ♠Q. She would do the same for him.

At other times, however, playing high as third hand is worse than futile. For example, partner leads the ♣7 against 4♠. Should you cover dummy's ♣J?

♣J 10 9 3

♣7   ♣Q 8 5 4

Partner's ♣7 cannot be low from strength (from ♣AK7 he would lead an honor), it can only be his highest (singleton, doubleton or tripleton). You cannot promote a trick by covering. If you cover, declarer has four club tricks. If you duck, unless partner's ♣7 is a singleton, declarer has only three club tricks. Play the ♣5 to start a high-low count signal. If on the next round you play the ♣4, partner will know you have four clubs, but declarer may think you have ♣54 doubleton and partner led from ♣Q87. Best of both worlds: informing partner while keeping declarer in the dark!

THIRD HAND QUIZ: UNDER THE BUS OR NOT?

In these problems, you are defending against 4♡ reached via an auction that is most unrevealing, starting with a 1♡ opening by the dealer on your left, with nothing but hearts bid throughout.

It might be 1♡-3♡; 4♡ ... or 1♡-2♡; 4♡ ... or 1♡-2♡; 3♡-4♡.

Partner leads the club shown, and declarer plays the underlined card from dummy. Choose your play!

(1)

	♣**J** 10 9 7 4	
♣6		♣Q 8 3

(2)

	♣**Q** J 4	
♣9		♣K 10 7 3

(3)

	♣7 6 4 **2**	
♣3		♣K 10 8 5

(4)

	♣Q **10** 9 4	
♣7		♣K 8 3 2

(5)

	♣J **3**	
♣8		♣K Q 9 2

ANSWERS

(1) ♣3. Partner's ♣6 cannot be low from honor-third, as he would lead an honor from ♣AK6. It can only be top of a tripleton, doubleton or singleton. You can promote nothing by covering. Ducking, however, may force declarer to block the suit.

(2) ♣3. Partner isn't underleading the ♣A. Declarer has the ♣A: don't throw your ♣K under it. Save the ♣K to cover dummy's *last* honor. Even the ♣7 may be too valuable to relinquish. You cannot promote a club trick for your side by covering. And if a "clever" declarer played an honor from dummy to induce you to throw your ♣K under a *singleton* ♣A, he'll soon regret it.

(3) ♣K. Partner's ♣3 *might* be a singleton, but it might also be from ♣Q93. Do not let declarer win a *preventable* second club trick with the ♣J if he has ♣AJ; instead, *promote* a trick for your partner's ♣Q. And if partner's ♣3 *is* a singleton declarer can finesse you out of all your clubs anyway.

(4) ♣3. Partner's ♣7 is his highest. He wouldn't lead it from ♣AJ7. Save your ♣K to beat dummy's card after the ♣A is gone.

(5) ♣Q. Partner's ♣8 might be second highest from length and weakness (e.g. ♣10874) but your ♣K will still stand guard behind dummy's now-bare ♣J if it is. By playing the ♣Q now, you keep declarer from winning a preventable trick with his likely ♣10 and you *promote* your ♣K to a winner. If you duck, both your club monarchs may be guillotined by ruffs in dummy.

THIRD HAND

NOT TOO HIGH

TO KEEP

COMMUNICATION

DEAL 77. THIRD HAND HIGH BUT NOT TOO HIGH

```
                        ♠ K J 10 7 3
                        ♡ 8 5
                        ◇ A 9 8 3
                        ♣ Q 6
        ♠ A 9 8 4                        ♠ 6 2
        ♡ 9 6 2                          ♡ A Q J 7 4
        ◇ Q 10 5                         ◇ 7 6 2
        ♣ 9 5 2                          ♣ 8 4 3
                        ♠ Q 5
                        ♡ K 10 3
                        ◇ K J 4
                        ♣ A K J 10 7
```

East doubled North's 2♡ Jacoby Transfer Bid for the lead but South chose to play game in notrumps rather than spades anyway. West led the ♡2. East won the ♡A and continued the ♡Q to drive out declarer's ♡K, but South waited for the third heart to win the ♡K. Good choice!

South shrugged his shoulders and led the ♠Q. He lucked out when West had the ♠A, for East had no entry to take the setting tricks with his two long hearts. "Overtrick!" said North when South soon claimed the rest.

Did South earn his good result, or did it spring from errors?

We'll ignore the subtleties of the auction that would have let South play 4♠, the safer game. South erred in the play by failing to try *all his chances*. A third diamond trick would see him home even if East had the ♠A.

So at Trick 4, cross to dummy's ♣Q to finesse the ◇J. If it wins, nine tricks without touching spades. If it loses, there's time enough to drive out the ♠A when West has that card too.

In the other room, East opened a loosey-goosy Weak 2♡ Bid. West led the ♡2 against 3NT. East won the ♡J and continued the ♡Q. South won the ♡K, but now *only* a diamond finesse could save him. It failed; down two.

DEAL 78. THIRD HAND: JUST ENCOURAGE

```
              ♠ A K J
              ♡ A 9
              ◇ J 10 7 5 2
              ♣ K Q 5
♠ 9 6 4 2                      ♠ 10 8 5
♡ 8 2                          ♡ K Q 7 6 3
◇ A 9 4                        ◇ K 8
♣ 9 8 6 2                      ♣ J 10 3
              ♠ Q 7 3
              ♡ J 10 5 4
              ◇ Q 6 3
              ♣ A 7 4
```

South bid 1NT over East's "favorable vulnerability" 1♡ overcall, and North raised to 3NT. West's ♡8 opening lead came through dummy's doubleton ♡A and South ducked Trick 1 to East's ♡Q. East's ♡6 ("original fourth highest") return dislodged dummy's ♡A.

Declarer went about establishing the tricks she needed in diamonds. East got in once to cash his second heart trick and set up a third, but he never got in again to cash it. North's diamonds came home and 3NT made.

Could 3NT have been defeated?

Yes. In the other room, *North* showed how. Huh? What's dummy got to do with it?

North wasn't dummy. His partner insisted on a good-15-to-18 HCP range for 1NT, and that's what he opened. With flat shape and four mediocre hearts, South eschewed Stayman. North was pleased to accept game when South invited with 2NT.

East led a fourth-highest ♡6 to declarer's ♡9. East ducked when declarer led the ◇2. West won the ◇K and returned hist last heart to drive out declarer's ♡A. East won the next diamond and cashed three hearts to beat the contract.

The first East could have obtained the same result by letting *dummy's* ♡9 hold Trick 1. Not an easy play!

DEAL 79. THE MONARCH OR THE KNAVE?

♠ Q 9 8 6
♡ 8
◊ Q 3
♣ A K 10 9 7 5

        ♠ J 7
        ♡ 9 7 6 5
        ◊ A 10 6
        ♣ 8 6 3 2

South	West	North	East	
2 ♣ (a)	Pass	2◊ (b)	Pass	(a) strong, artificial and forcing
3 ♡ (c)	Pass	4♣ (d)	Pass	(b) neutral ("waiting") response
6 ♡	All Pass			(c) sets trumps, asks specific aces
				(d) ♣A but no other

The auction was an unusual one, and bears further discussion.
"How would North show two aces?" "What would he do with none?"
Interesting, and we'd love to tell you---but not here.
At both tables, West led the ◊2 and declarer covered with dummy's ◊3.

In the Open Room, East won the ◊A and returned the ◊10. In the Closed Room, East inserted the ◊10. Who was right?

Frank Stockton wrote a fable called "The Lady or the Tiger?" We ask "The Monarch or the Knave?" Which diamond honor did declarer have?
Was it the Monarch, ♠AK ♡AKQJ1042 ◊K954 ♣void?
Or was it the Knave, ♠AK ♡AKQJ1042 ◊J954 ♣void?

In the Open Room, declarer won Trick 2 with dummy's ◊Q and threw the ◊9 on dummy's ♣A before drawing trump to claim his gambling slam.

In the Closed Room, East inferred South was void in clubs from his failure to use Blackwood. He played him for the Monarch. South won the ◊K and returned the ◊4 to East's ◊A. East shifted to the ♡9 to smother dummy's ♡8 and prevent a diamond ruff. West's ◊J8 took the last two tricks. Down two.

DEAL 80. THIRD HAND: HOW HIGH?

♠ K Q 7 5
♡ A 2
♢ 10 8 7 6
♣ K 4 3

　　　　　　　　♠ A 10 8 2
　　　　　　　　♡ 9 6 5
　　　　　　　　♢ void
　　　　　　　　♣ Q J 10 9 7 2

South opened a "Weak 2♡ Bid" and passed the 3♡ that North bid over West's 3♢ overcall. West led the ♠3 against 3♡, and declarer played the ♠5 from dummy.

In one room, East played the ♠10; in the other, East played the ♠A.

Who was right?

We put "Weak 2♡ Bid" in quote-marks because she ain't what she used to be. When Danny learned Weak Twos (1953), they were narrowly defined. One constraint was "One, two or three cards in the other major."

Is Danny the only one who still adheres to that as a guideline?

Not exactly. With ♠J964 ♡KQJ1043 ♢K2 ♣8, for example, four feeble spades and six stout hearts, even an old fuddy-duddy like Danny would open 2♡.

There's every clue that South has something like that here. If West had ♠Jxx, why would he lead spades? If South didn't have the ♠J, why would he play low from dummy?

Most significantly, *how could East hope to beat 3♡ unless West's ♠3 were singleton?*

So, up with the ♠A, return the ♠10 to show preference for diamonds, crossruff spades and diamonds, and when West turns up with the ♣A ... down two. Frosting on the cake! The East who ducked failed to ask the right questions; he got no dessert at all.

DEAL 81. THIRD HAND LOW

♠ 7 5 4
♡ A 10 8
♢ A 9 8 5
♣ A 5 2

♠ 8 2
♡ J 9 6 5 3 2
♢ J 6
♣ 10 8 7

♠ A K 10 6 3
♡ 7 4
♢ Q 7 3
♣ Q J 3

♠ Q J 9
♡ K Q
♢ K 10 4 2
♣ K 9 6 4

East's 1♠ overcall didn't keep South from jumping to 3NT, but it did fetch a spade lead from West. East took the first two spade tricks and led a third spade.

After winning Trick 3, declarer led to dummy's ♢A and floated dummy's ♢9, keeping the Danger Hand out. West won the ♢J, but now declarer had nine tricks: one spade, two clubs, and three in each red suit.

Could the defenders have done better?

Yes. In the other room, East ducked the first spade. Now both defenders were Danger Hands. After East's duck, declarer played him for a singleton quack in diamonds.

No such luck. East took one diamond and four spade tricks, down one.

DEAL 82. BOTH SIDES NOW

```
                    ♠ K 7 4
                    ♡ Q 7
                    ◇ Q J 2
                    ♣ K Q 10 7 3
  ♠ 10 6                           ♠ A Q 8 5 3
  ♡ 9 5 3 2                        ♡ 10 8 6 4
  ◇ 8 6 5 4                        ◇ 9 7 3
  ♣ A 9 2                          ♣ 4
                    ♠ J 9 2
                    ♡ A K J
                    ◇ A K 10
                    ♣ J 8 6 5
```

Don't ask us what the right lead from the West hand after a 1NT-3NT auction is. But this is one of the rare times we'd lead the ♠10, trying to find partner's suit. West's red-suit holdings seem to hold little promise.

Declarer played low from dummy. East asked the right question, "From what holdings might partner's ♠10 be?" As it might be from ♠109x but also from a doubleton, East played a thoughtful ♠8 to preserve the link between hands while encouraging a continuation.

South won the ♠J but was helpless to keep West from getting in with the ♣A. Another spade lead allowed East to run four spade tricks.

Did declarer do anything wrong to fail in a "30-point" 3NT?

Maybe, though we must credit East for his thoughtful play. In the other room South noticed what others might have missed- the ♠9. Reading West's ♠10 for a doubleton, he rose with dummy's ♠K at Trick 1.

Not only did the ♠9 speak loud and clear about West's holding, it provided a sure stopper. Had he held ♠J62, for example, he would have to fear that West's ♠10 was from ♠Q109x or longer.

So South played the ♠K from dummy. East didn't think his play required any thought. He smiled and said, "Aces are meant to take kings," as he played the ♠A. Now the defenders were helpless.

"Thank you, Mother Goose!" said South. What did he mean by that?

DEAL 83. THIS DUCK WON'T FLY

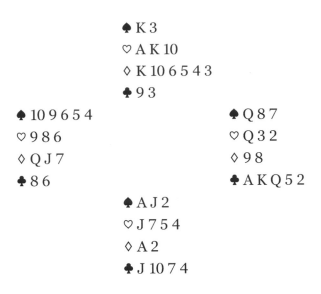

♠ K 3
♥ A K 10
♦ K 10 6 5 4 3
♣ 9 3

♠ 10 9 6 5 4
♥ 9 8 6
♦ Q J 7
♣ 8 6

♠ Q 8 7
♥ Q 3 2
♦ 9 8
♣ A K Q 5 2

♠ A J 2
♥ J 7 5 4
♦ A 2
♣ J 10 7 4

The carnage might have been great had South been able to double East's non-vul 2♣ overcall for penalties. But only a "Negative Double" was available, so he had to content himself with 2NT. North bid 3NT.

West led the ♣8 and East won the first three tricks with club honors. Then he looked to see where he could win the two more tricks he needed to beat 3NT. He looked in his hand, on the floor, and out the window.

They were nowhere to be found, so he continued with the ♣2.

South won the ♣J, ◊A and dummy's ◊K, then shrugged his shoulders and led dummy's ◊10, praying the missing ◊Q lay with West, the safe hand. His prayer was answered and he took the rest. Making 3NT.

Were the defenders helpless to beat 3NT?

Yes and no. East could rely on South for a club stopper. At the other table, East ducked Trick 1 and hoped West had a diamond stopper and a second club. When the other declarer cashed the A-K of diamonds, he went quietly down.

But even this prayer might not have sufficed, for declarer could have taken one club, three spades via a finesse, and two top diamonds before throwing East in with clubs. After running clubs, East would have had to lead from his remaining ♡Q32, giving declarer nine tricks the hard way.

DEAL 84. RINGO'S LAW

```
                    ♠ 6 4
                    ♡ J 8 5
                    ◊ Q J 9 7
                    ♣ Q 10 3 2
    ♠ 9 3                         ♠ K Q 10 8 5 2
    ♡ 9 7 6 4 3                   ♡ A 10 2
    ◊ A 3 2                       ◊ 4
    ♣ K 6 5                       ♣ 9 8 7
                    ♠ A J 7
                    ♡ K Q
                    ◊ K 10 8 6 5
                    ♣ A J 4
```

A queen-majority added to a jack-monopoly spells trouble for pairs who lower the old-fashioned standards, and North-South faced trouble when they reached 2NT after a 2◊ raise and East's 2♠ overcall.

However, Ringo's Law ("I get by with a little help from my friends!") may have saved them here. Can you see how?

West led the ♠9 to East's ♠Q, and declarer let it hold. East continued with an "original fourth highest" ♠8 that South won cheaply with the ♠J. He drove out the ◊A and wound up with an easy nine tricks, losing one trick in each suit. North and South each blamed the other for missing game.

"Never drop me in two notrump when we're vul at IMPs!"

"Couldn't you stretch a couple of points and *open* two notrump? Everybody's doin' it." "Who do you think I am? Little Eva?"

Did North-South miss a game or could East-West defeat 2NT?

In the other room, East-West defended 2NT on the same auction. West led the ♠9 and she overtook with the *ten* and said, "No cheap tricks."

"That's what *you* say," said South as he won the ♠J. He drove out West's ◊A, won the next spade with the ♠A and counted only seven tricks. He tried a desperate club finesse. West won the ♣K, put East in with the ♡A, and now the defenders had seven tricks. Down two!

DEAL 85. THIRD HAND NOT TOO
HIGH TO SAVE AN ENTRY

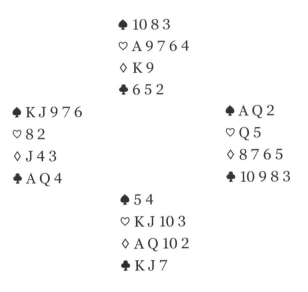

Danny claims never to have opened a bad 15-HCP 1NT in his life, but says he'd open a good-15-to-18-HCP 1NT with this South hand. Two psychiatrists think he is crazy. Two of them held the South cards in different rooms and opened 1◊. They got pushed to 3♡ after a 1♠ overcall, a "Negative Double" and a 2♠ raise. Each received a ♠7 lead.

In the Open Room, East found the excellent ♣10 shift after winning the ♠A. West captured declarer's ♣J with the ♣Q but unsure of the location of the ♠Q, he cashed the ♠K and ♣A. That was all for the defense, as hearts split 2-2.

How did the shrink who held the South cards in the Closed Room shrink his nine tricks into eight?

Well, maybe *he* didn't. Applying the Rule of 11, East at his table placed West with ♠KJ97x precisely and won Trick 1 with the ♠Q. Then, upon winning the first club, West returned the ♠6 confidently to put East in with the ♠A for another club lead through. Down one off the top.

What did we say earlier about third hand's normal play from AQx?

DEAL 86. USE YOUR ENTRY WHEN YOU CAN USE IT USEFULLY

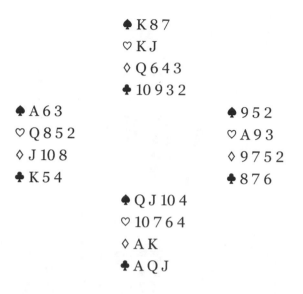

♠ K 8 7
♡ K J
◊ Q 6 4 3
♣ 10 9 3 2

♠ A 6 3
♡ Q 8 5 2
◊ J 10 8
♣ K 5 4

♠ 9 5 2
♡ A 9 3
◊ 9 7 5 2
♣ 8 7 6

♠ Q J 10 4
♡ 10 7 6 4
◊ A K
♣ A Q J

A 1NT-2NT-3NT auction gave the defenders a very good idea of the point-counts around the table. West might have gone passive with a ◊J opening lead, but passivity isn't as safe as advertised. Notrump play is a race to see which side can establish its tricks first. West's ♡2 opening lead looks pretty decent to us.

East captured dummy's ♡J with the ♡A and returned the ♡9 to drive out dummy's ♡K. Declarer lost a club finesse to West's ♣K. West could take only two more tricks, the ♠A and the ♡Q.

South's ♡10764 stood up as a second stopper in the suit. Limping home with nine tricks.

Could the defense have prevailed?

In the other room, East paused to think before playing to Trick 1. He had only one arrow in his quiver and he hated to use it before a suitable target came into view. From West's ♡2 lead East could read declarer for four hearts too.

If South's four hearts included the ♡10 without the ♡8, East could use his ♡A entry later to lead up to West's possible remaining ♡Q8.

Voila! East encouraged with the ♡9, and the defenders got three heart tricks to go with one trick in each of the black suits. Down one.

NOT
TOO HIGH:
MAKE DECLARER
WIN EARLY

DEAL 87. THIRD HAND: A NOT TOO HIGH CARD

We've all heard "third hand high." Defending against notrump, for example, one might, holding A Q x in third seat, win the ace and return the queen. Now declarer can duck the queen and take any finesses through the "Danger Hand."

So it is normal, almost routine, for a good defender to play the queen rather than the ace, keeping declarer in the dark. Declarer dare not duck lest the layout is:

x x

A J x x x   Q x x

K 10 x

And when the layout is actually ...

x x

J x x x x   A Q x

K 10 x

... your side gets the same four tricks, without your needing an outside entry to partner's hand.

A typical deal:

♠ 10 3
♡ Q 9 4
◊ A 7 5
♣ K J 9 8 2

♠ J 9 7 5 2   ♠ A Q 6
♡ J 8 5   ♡ 10 6 3
◊ Q 10 3   ◊ J 9 6 2
♣ 4 3   ♣ A 7 5

♠ K 8 4
♡ A K 7 2
◊ K 8 4
♣ Q 10 6

West leads the ♠5 against a notrump contract. If East plays the ♠A and continues the ♠Q, declarer gets ten tricks. If East plays the ♠Q *in tempo*, the defenders get five tricks first.

DEAL 88. GETTING YOUR NAME IN THE NEWSPAPER

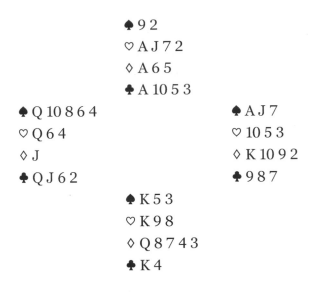

                        ♠ 9 2
                        ♡ A J 7 2
                        ◇ A 6 5
                        ♣ A 10 5 3
    ♠ Q 10 8 6 4   ♠ A J 7
    ♡ Q 6 4   ♡ 10 5 3
    ◇ J   ◇ K 10 9 2
    ♣ Q J 6 2   ♣ 9 8 7
                        ♠ K 5 3
                        ♡ K 9 8
                        ◇ Q 8 7 4 3
                        ♣ K 4

With both sides vulnerable, South responded 1◇ and then invited game by jumping to 2NT over North's 1♡ rebid. North raised to 3NT. West led the ♠6 and East played the ♠J. Fearing that West had led from the ♠A, South won the ♠K. Curtains! Declarer could no longer develop a second diamond trick for his ninth trick, and down he went. East got his name in a newspaper column for his brilliant play to Trick 1.

Or did he? Actually, we tricked you by showing you the two hands that East could not have seen without cheating. This was the actual deal:

                        ♠ 9 2
                        ♡ A J 7 2
                        ◇ A 6 5
                        ♣ A 10 5 3
    ♠ K 10 8 6 4 3   ♠ A J 7
    ♡ Q 6 4   ♡ 10 5 3
    ◇ J   ◇ K 10 9 2
    ♣ J 6 2   ♣ 9 8 7
                        ♠ Q 5
                        ♡ K 9 8
                        ◇ Q 8 7 4 3
                        ♣ K Q 4

Don't outsmart yourself. Unless you're *sure* South has the ♠K, win the ♠A. Remember, when South does have ♠Kxx, he'll often forget to duck the return. Sometimes he has ♠Kx and *can't* duck.

DEAL 89. COVER OF THE ROLLING STONE

```
                    ♠ A K 9 5 3
                    ♡ 8
                    ◇ A 10 9 6 3
                    ♣ 9 3                Willie
    ♠ Q 8 7                              ♠ J 6 4
    ♡ 7 6 5                              ♡ K 10 9 3
    ◇ 8 2                                ◇ Q J 7
    ♣ Q 8 6 4 2                          ♣ A J 5
                    ♠ 10 2
                    ♡ A Q J 4 2
                    ◇ K 5 4
                    ♣ K 10 7
```

West led the ♣4 against 3NT. Not satisfied with getting his name in the newspaper yesterday, East decided to try to get his picture on the cover of *The Rolling Stone*. Knowing that West just couldn't have an outside entry on the auction, he inserted a sly ♣J.

He didn't even look to see with which honor South took Trick 1 but started tapping his feet and singing, "Gonna buy five copies for my mother."

However, as you oughta know by now, we fooled you again. The actual deal:

```
                    ♠ A K 9 5 3
                    ♡ 8
                    ◇ A 10 9 6 3
                    ♣ 9 3                Willie
    ♠ 10 8 7                            ♠ J 6 4
    ♡ J 6 5                             ♡ K 10 9 3
    ◇ 8 2                               ◇ Q J 7
    ♣ K 10 6 4 2                        ♣ A J 5
                    ♠ Q 2
                    ♡ A Q 7 4 2
                    ◇ K 5 4
                    ♣ Q 8 7
```

Guess who apologized at the end of play. This time, we trust, you got it right. "Sorry," said South. "When they both threw hearts, I could have won all 13 tricks just by finessing Willie for the king of hearts."

DEAL 90. LOSING A TRICK EARLY

           ♠ A J 10 7
           ♡ 9 5 2
           ◊ 10
           ♣ A J 10 8 4

♠ 9 6 3   ♠ 8 5 4 2
♡ A 10 8 7 3   ♡ K J
◊ 9 8 7 2   ◊ K 6 5 3
♣ 6   ♣ K 7 3

           ♠ K Q
           ♡ Q 6 4
           ◊ A Q J 4
           ♣ Q 9 5 2

South reached 3NT via a Stayman auction. West led the ♡7 to East's ♡K and East returned the ♡J, expecting to drive out declarer's ♡A. But declarer's heart honor was the ♡Q, not the ♡A, and he withheld it.

East shifted to the ◊3. South, who had read the heart position correctly, rose with the ◊A to keep the Danger Hand out. If the club finesse worked, a diamond finesse was redundant. The club finesse lost and East cashed the ◊K, but that was all for the defenders, so 3NT rolled home.

"Look Ma," said East. I won all four of my honor cards." West scowled and said, "I'll see you in the woodshed after the game."

The East player in the other room won only one trick, but he beat 3NT. How could that be?

All became clear in the post mortem when East explained:

"I knew from the auction that my partner had at most four points, and two queens wouldn't suffice to beat three notrump. But ace-ten-eight-fifth of hearts was consistent with the bidding and opening lead. So I played for just that, and inserted the jack.

"Only a Martian would know to let me win it, but declarer's skin was brown, not green, so I knew he was an Earthling. After winning the queen of hearts, declarer lost a finesse to my club king. Partner overtook my king of hearts and ran the suit. Duck soup!"

DEAL 91. COUNTING PARTNER'S POINTS

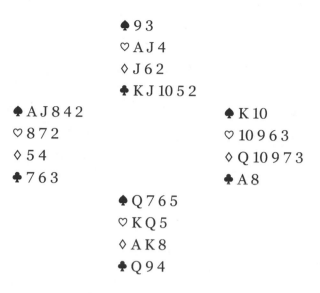

                    ♠ 9 3
                    ♡ A J 4
                    ◇ J 6 2
                    ♣ K J 10 5 2

♠ A J 8 4 2   ♠ K 10
♡ 8 7 2   ♡ 10 9 6 3
◇ 5 4   ◇ Q 10 9 7 3
♣ 7 6 3   ♣ A 8

                    ♠ Q 7 6 5
                    ♡ K Q 5
                    ◇ A K 8
                    ♣ Q 9 4

West led a fourth-highest ♠4 against 1NT-3NT and after winning the ♠K, East returned the ♠10. South played low and hoping that East had a third spade, West played the ♠2.

However, East was out of spades and declarer set up four club tricks to go with five top red-suit winners and make 3NT.

How did the declarer in the other room find a way to go down in 3NT?

There, East counted West for at most 5 or 6 HCP and at most five spades. At Trick 1, East played the ♠10. Declarer won the ♠Q and started clubs.

When East won and led the ♠K, West overtook with the ♠A and cashed three more spade tricks.

"I have to find an easier game," commented South.

DEAL 92. AND EVEN ONE MORE

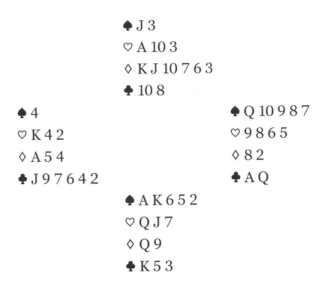

♠ J 3
♥ A 10 3
♦ K J 10 7 6 3
♣ 10 8

♠ 4
♥ K 4 2
♦ A 5 4
♣ J 9 7 6 4 2

♠ Q 10 9 8 7
♥ 9 8 6 5
♦ 8 2
♣ A Q

♠ A K 6 5 2
♥ Q J 7
♦ Q 9
♣ K 5 3

After North opened a Weak 2♦ Bid, South became declarer in 3NT, West led the ♣6 to East's ♣A and South ducked East's ♣Q continuation. East shifted to the ♥9, which went to South's ♥Q, West's ♥K and dummy's ♥A. Then declarer drove out West's ♦A and wound up with 10 tricks.

What happened in the other room?

In the Closed Room, North-South were playing Flannery, so North passed as dealer. South opened a questionable 1NT. North raised to 3NT. West also led the ♣6, but East played the ♣Q. South won the ♣K and started diamonds. West ducked twice and won the third diamond.

East realized that West's three higher clubs were the ♣J97 and discarded the ♣A to unblock. Then West ran clubs to beat 3NT two.

Anybody do anything wrong?

Yes, one of the Easts, but we don't know which. West might have had the hand shown, but he might also have had ...

     (b) ♠4 ♥K42 ♦954 ♣KJ9642,
     (c) ♠4 ♥K42 ♦954 ♣KJ7642
   or (d) ♠4 ♥K42 ♦954 ♣K976432.

We believe that the East who beat 3NT did wrong and the East who failed to beat 3NT did right. Bridge is often a game of probabilities, seldom certainties.

DEAL 93. THIRD HAND'S PLAY FROM EQUALS

```
                        ♠ A Q J
                        ♡ K J 10 9 2
                        ◇ Q 2
                        ♣ 7 5 3
        ♠ 10 8 7 6 4                      ♠ 5 2
        ♡ 7 6 5                           ♡ A Q 3
        ◇ 9                               ◇ A 10 8 7 6 4
        ♣ Q 10 8 2                        ♣ 9 4
                        ♠ K 9 3
                        ♡ 8 4
                        ◇ K J 5 3
                        ♣ A K J 6
```

In the old days, after North opened 1♡, South might have doubled East's 2◇ overcall for penalties But it's been decades since anyone played penalty doubles of low-level overcalls, so the best South could do was jump to 3NT.

West led the ◇9 to East's ◇A and discarded the ♠4 when East returned the ◇7 to dummy's ◇Q. Despite losing a finesse to East's ♡Q, declarer had an easy path to ten tricks.

Which diamond must East play to Trick 1 to beat 3NT?

Only the ◇10 will do.

Playing the ◇A on air gave declarer a third diamond stopper and a trick, as it turned dummy's ◇Q from a victim into a victor on the second round of the suit.
Playing an "encouraging" ◇8 would fail if declarer had the foresight to let West's ◇9 win, as West lacked a second diamond to lead.

Playing the ◇10 makes it futile for declarer to duck, as that would leave East on lead to continue with the ◇A and another. Now East's two heart entries suffice to set up the rest of his diamonds and cash them.

DEAL 94. THIRD HAND GOES EXTRA HIGH

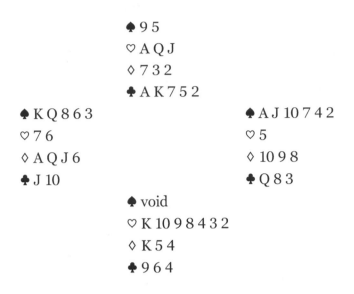

```
                        ♠ 9 5
                        ♡ A Q J
                        ◊ 7 3 2
                        ♣ A K 7 5 2
    ♠ K Q 8 6 3                         ♠ A J 10 7 4 2
    ♡ 7 6                               ♡ 5
    ◊ A Q J 6                           ◊ 10 9 8
    ♣ J 10                              ♣ Q 8 3
                        ♠ void
                        ♡ K 10 9 8 4 3 2
                        ◊ K 5 4
                        ♣ 9 6 4
```

South opened 3♡ on favorable vulnerability and North raised to 4♡. Neither East nor West had the wherewithal to save in 4♠."Save"? The favorable location of the ◊K would let 4♠ make.

West led the ♠K and East encouraged with the ♠J. South made a good play, discarding a club from his hand, a necessary precaution lest by ducking a club to establish the suit he let East, the Danger Hand, win to lead diamonds through him.

From there, declarer's path was easy. Ruff the spade continuation, draw trumps in two rounds and cash both top clubs. Then ruff a club, lead a third trump to dummy, and discard two diamonds on dummy's fourth and fifth clubs. Overtrick!

In the other room, South went down in 4♡. "I'll bet he ruffed West's king of spades," said Danny when Jim told him about this deal.

Is Danny psychic, or is he psychic?

Neither. "That's not what happened," said Jim. "At Trick One, East overtook the king of spades with the ace. Poor South was helpless.

If he ruffed the ace of spades, he would have to let East in with the queen of clubs later. Then a diamond shift through him would be fatal. If he discarded a club, the killing diamond shift would come immediately. He guessed to duck, and the defenders took the setting tricks promptly."

DESTROY
THE ENTRY
TO DUMMY

DEAL 95. THIRD HAND LOW TO KILL A DUMMY ENTRY

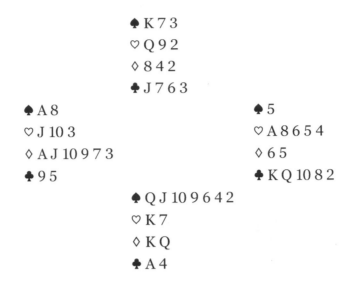

```
                    ♠ K 7 3
                    ♡ Q 9 2
                    ◇ 8 4 2
                    ♣ J 7 6 3
    ♠ A 8                          ♠ 5
    ♡ J 10 3                       ♡ A 8 6 5 4
    ◇ A J 10 9 7 3                 ◇ 6 5
    ♣ 9 5                          ♣ K Q 10 8 2
                    ♠ Q J 10 9 6 4 2
                    ♡ K 7
                    ◇ K Q
                    ♣ A 4
```

South declared 4♠ after a competitive auction. East's (misnamed) "Responsive Double" having promised hearts and clubs, West led the ♡J. When declarer dropped the ♡K under East's ♡A, dummy shook a finger at him and scolded, "Chest your cards!"

East shifted promptly to the ♣K. Declarer won the ♣A and led the ♡7. When West followed with the ♡3, declarer finessed dummy's ♡9. Then he discarded his club loser on the ♡Q. Making 4♠, losing only three aces.

When the match was over and West compared scores with her teammates, she saw that South had gone down in 4♠.

She shook a finger at him and said, "Didn't you unblock the heart king? You should read Dr J's book on Unblocking."

"No," he replied. "I won the heart king. You guys misdefended."

Why did he think so?

At his table, East ducked the opening lead. South won the ♡K and finessed dummy's ♡9 immediately. East won the ♡A at Trick 2 and shifted to the ♣K then. South won the ♣A and led a sneaky ♠J.

"You took the push to four spades on a jack-high suit? I don't think you would," said West as he rose with the ♠A. He returned a club and waited with the ◇A to take the setting trick.

DEAL 96. THIRD HAND LOW TO PRESERVE YOUR TRICK

```
                              ♠ Q J 10
                              ♡ 7 2
                              ◇ 8 3
                              ♣ A J 10 9 8 4
         ♠ 9 7 6 4 2                        ♠ K 5 3
         ♡ Q 6 3                            ♡ J 10 8 5
         ◇ Q 7 5                            ◇ A 6 4
         ♣ 7 3                              ♣ K 5 2
                              ♠ A 8
                              ♡ A K 9 4
                              ◇ K J 10 9 2
                              ♣ Q 6
```

South opened a slightly off-shape 1NT. North raised to 3NT, relying on his clubs as a source of tricks. West led the ♠4.

Reading West for ace-fifth, East covered dummy's ♠10 with the ♠K, planning to return a higher-of-two-remaining ♠5. An alert West would watch the spots, read him for ♠K53, and withhold the ♠A to preserve it as an entry.

Oops! Declarer captured East's ♠K with the ♠A, floated the ♣Q, and when it won, repeated the club finesse. This time it lost, but declarer had 10 tricks even without guessing diamonds.

Could the defenders have done better?

In the other room, West led the ♠7, second-highest from length and weakness. That made it easy for East to play the ♠5 to Trick 1. After winning dummy's ♠10, declarer let dummy's ◇8 ride to West's ◇Q.

West's ♠9 continuation clarified the spade position for East, who ducked again. Declarer won the ♠A and floated ♣Q which won. Now South could have made nine tricks by reverting to diamonds.

However. accustomed to matchpoints where overtrick greed can be rewarding, he repeated the seemingly successful club finesse and went down. "I risked only one trick to gain five," he told his teammates in the post mortem.

DEAL 97. THIRD HAND SAVES A HIGH CARD TO KILL A DUMMY ENTRY

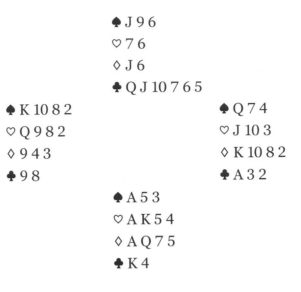

♠ J 9 6
♡ 7 6
◇ J 6
♣ Q J 10 7 6 5

♠ K 10 8 2
♡ Q 9 8 2
◇ 9 4 3
♣ 9 8

♠ Q 7 4
♡ J 10 3
◇ K 10 8 2
♣ A 3 2

♠ A 5 3
♡ A K 5 4
◇ A Q 7 5
♣ K 4

South opened 2NT and North responded 3♣, which they played as a puppet to 3NT (!). West led the ♠2 against 3NT and declarer played the ♠9 from dummy.

"Trying for a cheap trick? Not through me!" said East, covering with the ♠Q. South won the ♠A and led the ♣K. East ducked the first club, but when West followed to the second, East knew it was safe to win the ♣A.

East shifted to the ♡J. South won and led another spade. West rose with the ♠K and continued hearts. South won, crossed to dummy's ♠J, and ran the rest of the clubs. The ◇A provided an overtrick.

"Maybe we'll win one IMP," said East. "Mr. Conservative over here could have made an eleventh trick with a simple diamond finesse."

When they compared scores, instead of winning one IMP, East's team lost *13*. How could that happen?

In the other room, North raised South's 2NT opening to 3NT. When
South covered West's ♠2 opening lead with dummy's ♠9, East saw that she needed to keep dummy's ♠J from becoming an entry to dummy's long clubs. So she ducked.

Now dummy had no outside entry. When East ducked the first club and won the second, declarer had only seven tricks: one club and two tricks in each of the other suits. Down two, minus 200.

DEAL 98. KEEPING DECLARER FROM DUMMY

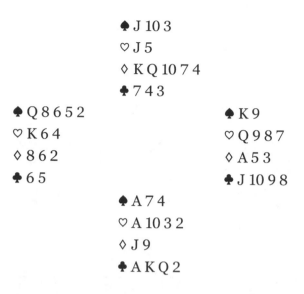

After North responded 1◊ and rebid 2◊, South jumped to 3NT. West led the ♠5. East covered dummy's ♠J with the ♠K.

"Maybe I should have played the ten from dummy," said South as he captured East's ♠K with the ♠A. "The ten's an honor too." answered East."

West showed count when declarer led the ◊J followed by the ◊9, so East knew to duck the first diamond. He captured dummy's ◊10 with his ◊A on the next round. Eventually, dummy's ♠10 served as an entry to dummy's diamonds. An easy ten tricks.

However, in the other room, 3NT failed. Why?

There East stared at dummy's diamonds and was scared. Whether West's lead was from the ♠A or ♠Q (he couldn't have both on the auction),
dummy's ♠10 would be an entry if East covered the ♠J. But not if he ducked.

So he held up his ♠K at Trick 1. Upon receiving a count signal from West when declarer led diamonds, he held up the ◊A one round also.

Declarer could never reach dummy, and three of dummy's beautiful diamonds went to waste.

USING THE
RULE OF ELEVEN
AS A GUIDE FOR
DEFENDING

DEAL 99. THIRD HAND DECISIONS
USING THE RULE OF ELEVEN

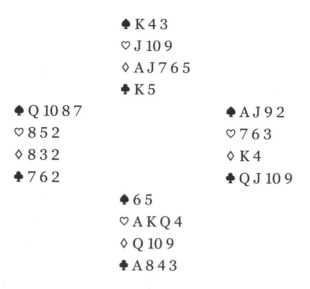

♠ K 4 3
♥ J 10 9
♦ A J 7 6 5
♣ K 5

♠ Q 10 8 7
♥ 8 5 2
♦ 8 3 2
♣ 7 6 2

♠ A J 9 2
♥ 7 6 3
♦ K 4
♣ Q J 10 9

♠ 6 5
♥ A K Q 4
♦ Q 10 9
♣ A 8 4 3

South opened 1NT and North bid 3NT. West led the ♠7 and declarer played the ♠3 from dummy. Reading West for the ♠Q, East played the ♠J, confident that it would win, perhaps overconfident for West's might have led from ♠1087. However, West had no reason to lead from any suit shorter than four, so West likely had the ♠Q.

When East's ♠J won, he counted the HCP. West couldn't have any other. East exited with the ♣Q. South won the ♣A and lost a finesse to East's ♦K. The best East could do was cash the ♠A to hold declarer to one overtrick. "Almost missed a slam, partner," said North.

Was North's post-mortem right?

Yes and no. East, who had flunked arithmetic in the second grade, misused the assets he had, which included the precious ♠2. The relevant number was 11.

Applying the Rule of 11, East could count four spades higher than West's ♠7. He *could see four between dummy and his own hand.* South couldn't have any card higher than the seven.

By playing the ♠2 at Trick 1, East could keep West on lead for another spade through to win the first four tricks in spades. Then he could wait to take the setting trick with the ♦K.

DEAL 100. THIRD HAND DECISIONS
USING THE RULE OF ELEVEN

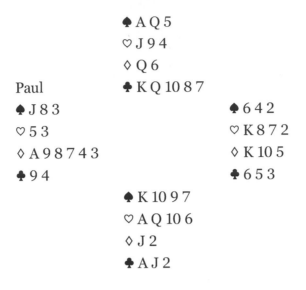

```
                          ♠ A Q 5
                          ♡ J 9 4
                          ◊ Q 6
        Paul              ♣ K Q 10 8 7
        ♠ J 8 3                          ♠ 6 4 2
        ♡ 5 3                            ♡ K 8 7 2
        ◊ A 9 8 7 4 3                    ◊ K 10 5
        ♣ 9 4                            ♣ 6 5 3
                          ♠ K 10 9 7
                          ♡ A Q 10 6
                          ◊ J 2
                          ♣ A J 2
```

Paul led the ◊7 after a 1NT-3NT auction. Declarer played low from dummy. East played the ◊10, keeping the ◊K behind dummy's ◊Q. It's still sitting there. South won the ◊J, then four spades and five clubs, and with ten tricks home the greedy declarer finessed in hearts to take all 13 tricks.

"With 22 points you opened only *one* notrump?" said North. "Why don't you bid our grand slams?"

"Because I had only 15 points and one notrump was all we could make," replied South.

Huh? Was she right? And why was West, a winner of the 1957 Intercollegiate Championship, tearing up his cards one by one?

The Rule of 11 told East that South had one card higher than the ◊7. Which honor East plays matters only if that card is the ◊A or the ◊J. Any clues?

Yes, *two*. Wouldn't South try the ◊Q if he had the ◊A? And the subtler clue: from a suit headed by ◊J987, West's normal lead is the ◊9, top of an internal sequence from a weak suit, headed by at best the jack.

DEAL 101. WHO'S TO BLAME?

```
                    ♠ K 9 3
                    ♡ J 8 3
                    ♢ J 8 2
                    ♣ A Q 5 4
   ♠ J 8 2                          ♠ 10 7 6 5
   ♡ 10 7 4                         ♡ 9 6 5
   ♢ A Q 7 4                        ♢ K 9 3
   ♣ 10 7 2                         ♣ K 9 6
                    ♠ A Q 4
                    ♡ A K Q 2
                    ♢ 10 6 5
                    ♣ J 8 3
```

After a 1NT-3NT auction, West led the ♢4. Declarer has only eight top tricks, so the contract should hinge on a club finesse. As the ♣K is offside, 3NT should fail but it didn't. At Trick 1, declarer played the ♢2 from dummy. What should East play? The ♢9 or K with the jack in dummy? He played the ♦9. South won the ♢10. With eight more tricks he made 3NT.

Whose fault was this disaster?

East knew from the spot cards West's ♢4 was from a four-card suit. If West had ♢10xxx or ♢Q10xx, then East had to play the ♢9 to keep dummy's ♢J from scoring. If West had ♢AQxx, then East had to play the ♢K. That's 2-to-1 odds in favor of East's actual ♢9 play. Or is it?

The case for the ♢9 was much stronger. Leads from five-card suits headed by an ace can develop *two* long-card tricks. Leads from four-card suits headed by the ace can develop only one long-card trick and often none so leading from ace-fourth usually sacrifices a trick in the suit.

A lead from AQxxx is a reasonable investment, but from AQxx should be chosen only when all other suits look worse.

All blame to West! In the other room, a sensible West chose the safest lead she could find, the ♡10. Declarer won but had only eight tricks.

DEAL 102. RULE OF ELEVEN AND COUNT THE HIGH CARDS

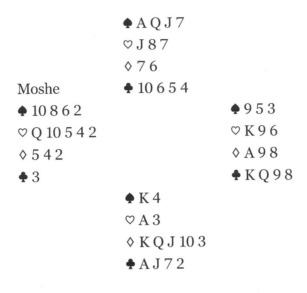

```
                        ♠ A Q J 7
                        ♡ J 8 7
                        ◊ 7 6
Moshe                   ♣ 10 6 5 4
♠ 10 8 6 2                               ♠ 9 5 3
♡ Q 10 5 4 2                             ♡ K 9 6
◊ 5 4 2                                  ◊ A 9 8
♣ 3                                      ♣ K Q 9 8
                        ♠ K 4
                        ♡ A 3
                        ◊ K Q J 10 3
                        ♣ A J 7 2
```

East's third-seat 1♣ opening did not keep South from reaching 3NT. n West lead the ♡4. Declarer played low from dummy and captured East's ♡K with the ♡A. South started diamonds. East won the second diamond with the ◊A and returned the ♡9. Declarer soon claimed 11 tricks.

East said, "If I hadn't remembered Mother Goose's "Always return your partner's lead!' that tricky Moshe might have taken *twelve* tricks."
"And of 'Third hand high!' you say nothing?" sighed West.

What did West mean by that?

The auction precluded West's having both the ♡A and the ♡Q. To have any chance of beating 3NT, West needed to have five hearts. The Rule of 11 marked South with only one heart honor, almost surely the ♡A on the auction.
Mother Goose was wrong. A better rule: "Third hand *just high enough* to do the necessary jobs." Here East had two jobs to do. First to keep declarer from winning a preventable trick, and second, to prevent dummy's ♡J becoming a third-round stopper. The ♡9 was the card to do both jobs efficiently.
In the other room, East played a thoughtful ♡9 at Trick 1. The defenders took their five tricks to beat 3NT long before declarer could claim the rest.

DEAL 103. GOING VERY LOW

```
                    ♠ Q 10 5
                    ♡ Q 9 5
                    ◇ A K 3
Moshe               ♣ Q 10 8 3      Millie
♠ K 8 2                             ♠ 7 6 4
♡ J 8 7 6 3                         ♡ K 10 2
◇ 7 5 4                             ◇ 10 9 8 6
♣ A 2                              ♣ 9 6 4
                    ♠ A J 9 3
                    ♡ A 4
                    ◇ Q J 2
                    ♣ K J 7 5
```

It was another dull 1NT-3NT auction, and Millie had another dull, flat 3-HCP hand. Moshe led the ♡6 and declarer played low from dummy. Taking care to preserve the ♡K behind dummy's ♡Q, Millie played the ♡10, which sufficed to drive out declarer's ♡A.

South drove out West's ♣A and applying "Restricted Choice," covered West's ♡3 continuation with dummy's ♡9. Millie won the ♡K, the second trick for the defense, and returned the ♡2, but declarer came home with one spade, two hearts, and three tricks in each minor.

"*Now* what did I do wrong?" asked Millie on seeing Moshe grimace.

Sighing, he replied, "Dummy had *two* significant hearts for which you needed to preserve covers, the queen *and* nine. From my fourth-highest lead, you could tell declarer had only one higher heart.

If it were the seven or eight, he would probably have tried dummy's queen as his best chance. So your best bet was the deuce. Then you could win both the ten and the king of hearts before shifting to spades. Down two if declarer finesses you for the king of spades to try to make.".

DEAL 104. THIRD HAND RULE OF ELEVEN

```
                       ♠ K 7 6
                       ♡ K 5 4
                       ◇ A 6 3 2
    Post-Mortimer      ♣ Q 7 5
    ♠ A Q 10 9 8                   ♠ J 5 3
    ♡ 8                            ♡ 10 7 2
    ◇ J 8 7                        ◇ K 9 5 4
    ♣ J 8 6 2                      ♣ A 10 9
                       ♠ 4 2
                       ♡ A Q J 9 6 3
                       ◇ Q 10
                       ♣ K 4 3
```

After a 1♡ opening and a 1♠ overcall, South reached 4♡. West led the ♣2 and East won the ♣A. East shifted to spades but no matter what East led to Trick 2, declarer made 4♡ easily, losing one trick in each suit but hearts.

"Can't you count?" asked perpetually exasperated Post-Mortimer Snide.

In the other room four hearts was defeated. How?
Let's hear it from Mortimer.

"My deuce-lead denied a fifth club, so you know declarer has three or four. Did you have to take your ace on the first round? All you have to do is play the nine like a normal human being.

If I have both missing honors, king and jack, we'll win three club tricks. If I have one of them, we'll win two club tricks. You found the only way for us to win only one.

"You can't stop declarer from scoring a club trick if he has either missing honor in his hand, but you can stop dummy's queen from scoring. Just do it! I tied your ace of clubs to a leash by leading fourth highest, so he isn't about to run away."

What would we do without you, Mort? We'd have to write our own analyses. But thank God there aren't too many of you.

Else we'd be out of a job.

DEAL 105. THIRD HAND UNNECESSARILY HIGH (RULE OF ELEVEN)

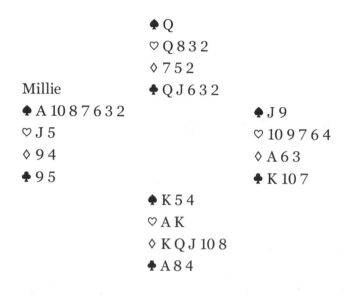

♠ Q
♡ Q 8 3 2
◇ 7 5 2
♣ Q J 6 3 2

Millie
♠ A 10 8 7 6 3 2
♡ J 5
◇ 9 4
♣ 9 5

♠ J 9
♡ 10 9 7 6 4
◇ A 6 3
♣ K 10 7

♠ K 5 4
♡ A K
◇ K Q J 10 8
♣ A 8 4

West's "favorable vulnerability" 3♠ opening forced South to gamble 3NT with a hand he'd planned to open 2NT. West led the ♠7.

Winning dummy's ♠Q, declarer started diamonds. East won the second diamond and returned the ♠J. Declarer ducked and West could not afford to overtake.

When his ♠J won, East exclaimed, "I'm glad you talked me into playing Upside-Down Signals, Millie! Playing old-fashioned signals, I'd have thrown my precious jack of spades under dummy's queen to show count, and I wouldn't have taken a trick with it now." Millie grimaced.

East shifted to the ♣7. South shrugged his shoulders and played low. When Millie followed with the ♣5, dummy's ♣J won and declarer cashed out for nine tricks. Millie is still sitting there with her spades as you read this.

How could the defenders have preserved their transportation?

Fourth-highest leads and the Rule of 11 can help again. Seven from eleven leaves four. East can see three of the four in dummy and his hand at Trick 1. That leaves declarer with only one spade higher than the ♠7, surely the ♠A or ♠K on the auction.

If it's the ♠K, East must unblock the ♠J to lead the ♠9 through declarer's remaining ♠Kx up to West's remaining ♠A10xxxx.

THIRD HAND: ATTITUDE, COUNT, SUIT PREFERENCE OR WHAT?

SIGNALING PRIORITIES

Nobody knows who designed the American Contract Bridge League's official convention card. Maybe he was too ashamed to put his name on it.

We won't discuss any of its shortcomings here except this one. It asks players to indicate their "primary signal to partner's leads" as either *attitude, count,* or *suit preference.* Want to guess which of these is right?

While you're thinking about that, here's an easier question. What color is *homo sapiens?* Like so many of the questions we are called upon to answer in school exams and the "forms" that have proliferated in recent decades, we'll offer multiple choices. Check one, please:

YELLOW_____   WHITE_____   BROWN_____

Danny wanted to answer "RED," which covers not only Native Americans but also those of us who sunbathe on the beaches of Miami and Los Angeles. Alas, that was not one of the choices offered. So he spent hours trying to figure out which was the smaller lie, "yellow" or "brown," until he decided to flip a mental coin ... only to have it land on edge. Why can't mental coins be as decisive as metal coins of silver and gold, copper and nickel, which always land heads or tails?

Back to more important stuff, what to signal at Trick 1. Danny finds this question easier. *Don't* signal unless you can afford to.

Play the right card, just as you would if you were declarer, with one important exception: as declarer you normally seek to conceal information, but as a defender you normally seek to reveal information about your hand ... except when you deem that information more helpful to declarer than to partner. Often, merely playing the right card will tell your partner *what he needs to know.*

We've just let the cat out of the bag. Tell partner *what he needs to know.* Usually, that's whether you'd welcome a continuation of the suit he led; this is not quite the same as "attitude," for you may have a lovely holding in the suit led but desperately need partner to switch to another.

Conversely, you may have an utterly worthless holding in the suit partner led but fear the "obvious" shift. When your attitude toward a suit is, or will soon be, obvious, your count may become important. Finally, when partner may hold the trick but have no card left in the suit to lead again, you may be able to signal suit preference to tell him how to try to put you in.

DEAL 106. THIRD HAND HIGH? NOT WHEN COUNT IS MORE IMPORTANT

Tina
♠ A K 10 9
♡ 10 7 6
♢ Q J 10 9
♣ J 2

♠ 8 5
♡ A Q 9 5 4
♢ K 2
♣ 8 6 4 3

♠ J 7 6 3
♡ 8 3 2
♢ 7 4
♣ K 10 9 5

♠ Q 4 2
♡ K J
♢ A 8 6 5 3   Danny
♣ A Q 7

South reached 3NT after North's Stayman. West led the ♡5 and declarer played the ♡6 from dummy. Dummy, the most voluptuous brunette East had ever seen at a bridge club, turned to him and begged sweetly: "My six, please stay off it!"

East refused to be corrupted. He covered with the ♡8, saying, "Sorry, Tina." Declarer won the ♡J, crossed to dummy's ♠K, and floated dummy's ♢Q. Upon winning the ♢K, West was unsure how to continue.

Picturing declarer with ♠ Qxx ♡ KJx ♢ Axxx ♣ KQx, he shifted to a top-of-nothing ♣8, trying to reach East for a heart lead through.

Soon declarer had 10 tricks.

How should the defenders have beaten 3NT?

Danny, Southeast, turned to his kibitzee and said, "When a woman as beautiful as Tina begs you to do something, obey!" Was Danny kidding?

No. He was criticizing East obliquely and kindly. From East's vantage point, he could virtually see South's heart holding as two bare honors, ♡AQ, ♡AJ or ♡KJ, but West could not unless East signaling *count*. The ♡2 was perfectly suited for that job. Then on regaining the lead, West could tell that South's ♡K would fall under the ♡A, and he'd run hearts to beat 3NT.

DEAL 107. THIRD HAND ATTITUDE

```
                        ♠ K Q 5
                        ♡ 6 3
                        ◊ A K Q 10 9 8
                        ♣ 9 4
        ♠ 3 2                              ♠ 8
        ♡ A K 8 7                          ♡ Q 10 4 2
        ◊ J 7 4                            ◊ 6 5 3
        ♣ A Q J 10                         ♣ 7 6 5 3 2
                        ♠ A J 10 9 7 6 4
                        ♡ J 9 5
                        ◊ 2
                        ♣ K 8
```

South opened a vulnerable 3♠ as dealer. West doubled and North raised to 4♠, hoping South didn't have four fast losers in clubs and hearts.

Playing Patriarch Opening Leads, whereby a king promises the queen, West led the ♡A. East encouraged with the ♡10, whereupon West cashed the ♡K and wondered, "What now?"

Dummy's intimidating diamonds provided the answer. West cashed the ♣A and continued the ♣Q, hoping that West had the ♣K. Declarer won, drew trumps, and claimed his contract.

How could West have known to unscramble his side's four tricks?

In the other room, the contract was the same. West saw East's ♡10 at Trick 1 and stopped to think *before* leading to Trick 2.

Ruling out as impossible that East had a doubleton and was signaling the ability to overruff dummy, West led the ♡7 to Trick 2. East won the ♡Q and shifted to clubs. The defenders took the setting tricks before declarer could catch his breath.

DEAL 108. ATTITUDE TOWARDS A CONTINUATION, NOT THE SUIT

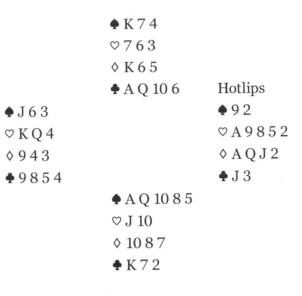

```
                    ♠ K 7 4
                    ♡ 7 6 3
                    ◊ K 6 5
                    ♣ A Q 10 6      Hotlips
        ♠ J 6 3                     ♠ 9 2
        ♡ K Q 4                     ♡ A 9 8 5 2
        ◊ 9 4 3                     ◊ A Q J 2
        ♣ 9 8 5 4                   ♣ J 3
                    ♠ A Q 10 8 5
                    ♡ J 10
                    ◊ 10 8 7
                    ♣ K 7 2
```

Good brakes let South stop in 3♠ after he overcalled 1♠. West led the ♡K, showing the ♡Q. East expressed his liking for hearts with an encouraging ♡9. West continued the ♡Q and East a thoughtful ♡8, indicating his preference for diamonds.

West shifted to the ◊9. East won the ◊J, but then could do no better than tap declarer with the ♡A. After ruffing, South drew trumps and took the ♣A and ♣K. As East's ♣J fell, South continued with a club to dummy's ♣Q and discarded a diamond on dummy's ♣10. Making 3♠.

In the other room, 3♠ failed. Do you see how?

East realized before playing to Trick 1 that she needed West to lead through dummy's ◊K65 *twice*. West had to shift to diamonds now, *before* cashing the ♡Q, his only other entry. Hotlips liked hearts but she craved diamonds.

She played the ♡2 at Trick 1, discouraging a heart continuation and leaving it to West to figure out the right shift. It was not hard for West to figure out which unbid suit to lead. He led the ◊9. Declarer played low from dummy, East won and put West back in with the carefully-preserved ♡Q for a second diamond lead through dummy's guarded ◊K.

The defenders took the first five tricks. Down one. As she marked +50 on her scorecard, Hotlips picked up all her hearts and kissed them to reassure them of her love. Especially the ♡2.

DEAL 109. DON'T WHISPER WHEN YOU CAN SHOUT

```
                    ♠ K 7 6 5
                    ♡ K 7 6 2
                    ◊ K 6
                    ♣ Q 10 8
        ♠ J 9 3                      ♠ A Q 10 8
        ♡ 9                          ♡ J 5
        ◊ Q J 8 5 4 3 2              ◊ 10 9 7
        ♣ J 5                        ♣ A K 3 2
                    ♠ 4 2
                    ♡ A Q 10 8 4 3
                    ◊ A
                    ♣ 9 7 6 4
```

East opened 1♣ in second seat and wound up defending against South's 3♡. West led the ♣J. East captured dummy's ♣Q with the ♣K, cashed the ♣A, and returned the ♣3 for West to ruff.

What now? The ♣2 was still outstanding, but so was the ♣9. Though aware that when giving a ruff, a defender tries to show suit preference, West could not tell whether East's ♣3 was his higher or lower. Or it might well have been his middle from ♣932. So diamonds or spades?

There was no need to guess what the whispering ♣3 showed. East had shouted preference for ... *diamonds*. Accordingly. West led the ◊Q. South won the ◊A, drew trumps with the ♡A and ♡K, threw a spade on dummy's ◊K, and lost only one more trick, a spade at the end. Making 3♡.

How did the defense solve this problem in the other room?

In the other room against the same contract, East realized Trick 1 offered his only opportunity to shout suit preference. Thinking ahead to West's Trick 4 problem, East played "high-low" on the first two clubs, ♣A then ♣K. West read the loud-and-clear message and shifted to the ♠J at Trick 4.
Result: down one.

DEAL 110. DANNY'S APRIL FOOLS DAY PRANK

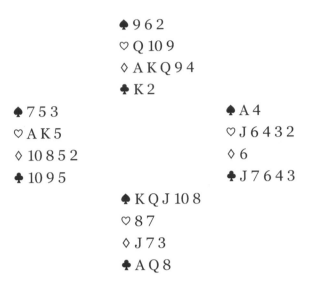

```
              ♠ 9 6 2
              ♡ Q 10 9
              ◇ A K Q 9 4
              ♣ K 2
♠ 7 5 3                        ♠ A 4
♡ A K 5                        ♡ J 6 4 3 2
◇ 10 8 5 2                     ◇ 6
♣ 10 9 5                       ♣ J 7 6 4 3
              ♠ K Q J 10 8
              ♡ 8 7
              ◇ J 7 3
              ♣ A Q 8
```

It was April 1. Danny slipped a deal from 64 years earlier into the boards. Back then, South had opened 1♠ and rebid 2♠ over North's 2◇ response. North had to guess which game to bid, 3NT or 4♠, and guessed 4♠. West led the ♡K, showing either the ♡A or the ♡Q.

Do you see how the defenders beat 4♠?

East played the ♡J. Surely East didn't hope for a heart ruff, as South wouldn't have suppressed a topless *five*-card heart suit to rebid spades. East's jack of hearts was an "Alarm Clock" play begging for a shift to the "unobvious" suit. West duly shifted to the ◇8. East won the first trump and put West in with a heart to receive a diamond ruff and beat 4♠.

That was then, but now, using Two-Over-One Game-Forcing, North could continue forcing with 2NT. With a balanced hand, South raised to 3NT and became dummy. This time the opening lead came from East, the ♡3. West played ♡K, ♡A, ♡5. North made 3NT without touching spades.

Do you see how the defenders might have beaten 3NT?

Perhaps. At Trick 1, West "falsecards" the ♡A, ostensibly denying the ♡K and fooling everyone. Declarer plays the ♡10, fooling no one. West returns the ♡5 and declarer finesses the ♡9. East wins the ♡J and persists with the ♡6, suit-preference for spades. West wins the ♡K and puts East in with the ♠A to cash two more hearts. Down two. Sure!

DEAL 111. ATTITUDE TOWARDS WHAT?

<pre>
                    ♠ K 10 8 4
                    ♡ A Q J 3
                    ◊ Q 9 3
                    ♣ 7 3
    ♠ 3   ♠ A J 9
    ♡ 10 8 6 4   ♡ 7 5 2
    ◊ A K 8 7 6   ◊ 10 5 2
    ♣ 6 5 2   ♣ Q 9 8 4
                    ♠ Q 7 6 5 2
                    ♡ K 9
                    ◊ J 4
                    ♣ A K J 10
</pre>

West had too little playing strength to intervene over South's 1♠ opening. North and South were using Jacoby Forcing Raises, triggered by North's 2NT, requiring South to show a singleton or void by bids at the three-level. His jump to 4♠ showed a balanced minimum, a feature of Jacoby that distinguishes them from other kinds of artificial 2NT raises.

West led the ◊A, normally showing the ◊K in his modern methods.

With three low diamonds, the worst possible holding, East played a discouraging ◊2. Envisioning declarer's 5=2=2=4 hand pattern exactly, West shifted to the ♡8, second highest from length and weakness, hoping to ensure a trick for East's possible ♡Kxx before declarer could set up dummy's ◊Q for a heart discard.

Oops! South's doubleton heart included the ♡K, and three rounds of hearts let him discard the ◊J. He lost only two more tricks to East's good trumps, and made 4♠.

Could the defenders have averted this misadventure?

Yes. In the other room, after the same auction, East realized that he had two trump tricks coming. So he feigned a doubleton by playing the ◊10 to Trick 1, encouraging West to cash the ◊K. That was all he needed to *set the contract*.

DEAL 112. DON'T MUMBLE WHEN YOU CAN SHOUT

```
                        ♠ Q J 7
                        ♡ Q 9 8 6
                        ◇ A Q
                        ♣ 9 8 5 2
        ♠ A K 9 4                       ♠ 10 5 3 2
        ♡ 2                             ♡ A 10 7 3
        ◇ 10 9 8 2                      ◇ 6 4 3
        ♣ Q 10 4 3        Moshe         ♣ 7 6
                        ♠ 8 6
                        ♡ K J 5 4
                        ◇ K J 7 5
                        ♣ A K J
```

Against 4♡ reached via Stayman, West led the ♠A, normally showing the ♠K in his partnership. East played the ♠5 and South, the notorious falsecarder Moshe, played the ♠8.

West was puzzled. The ♠5 could be the start of a high-low from ♠52 or ♠53. but it could also be low from ♠1065. Finally an "Aha!" moment. Why would Moshe falsecard the ♠8 from ♠10862 or ♠10863? Why not the ♠10? Applying "Restricted Choice," West shifted to the ◇10.

End of the defense! Winning in dummy, declarer led low to the ♡K and back to dummy's ♡Q. East won the ♡A and continued diamonds, but now declarer was able pick up trumps and come down to ♠6 and ♣KJ. Thrown in with his ♠K, West had to concede the contract.

Could the defenders have found a fourth trick?

Yes, as East might have discerned from his good trump spots. In the other room, East shouted "Please continue!" with a loud ♠10 at Trick 1. West continued with the ♠K then the ♠4. Declarer discarded the ♣J and like his counterpart started trumps by leading to his ♡K and back to dummy's ♡Q. East won the ♡A and led a fourth spade to West's dismay.

South's dismay was greater still. If he ruffed with the ♡6 from his remaining ♡J6, East's ♡10 would score. If he ruffed with dummy's ♡8 or ♡9, East's ♡7 would score. Down one either way.

"Sorry, partner," said East. "I had two spades mixed with my clubs."

DEAL 113. THIRD HAND GIVES FALSE COUNT AGAIN

```
                        ♠ Q J 3
                        ♡ K J 4 2
                        ◊ Q 9 2
                        ♣ J 4 3
        ♠ K 9 7 6 5                        ♠ 10 4
        ♡ A 7                              ♡ 9 8 6 3
        ◊ J 7 5                            ◊ K 4 3
        ♣ 9 8 6        Post-Mortimer       ♣ A 7 5 2
                        ♠ A 8 2
                        ♡ Q 10 5
                        ◊ A 10 8 6
                        ♣ K Q 10
```

After his Stayman 2♣, North bid 3NT. West led the ♠6 to dummy's ♠J. East followed with the ♠4 and South, Post-Mortimer Snide, played the ♠2.

With three suits to develop, declarer started diamonds by letting dummy's ◊9 ride to West's ◊J. Hoping a second spade would dislodge South's ♠A, West continued with the ♠5, but dummy's ♠Q won.

Upon finishing diamonds by finessing again and knocking out the ♡A, declarer had nine of the first 11 tricks, three in every suit but clubs. and when East turned up with the ♣A at Trick 12, South made an overtrick.

Post-Mortimer turned to West and said graciously, "Thank you for your second spade lead. Otherwise, I could never have made it."

Whose fault? Was Mortimer right? In the other room, 3 NT went down.

No, as usual, Post-Mortimer directed his sarcasm---er, *charm*---at the wrong target. It was East who had earned it. When East couldn't top dummy's ♠J at Trick 1, his attitude toward spades was known, but his spade length wasn't. So his next priority was count.

The ♠10 would have done the job, showing two. Then West would know to shift to the ♣9. On winning the ♣A, East could return the ♠4 to set up the rest of the suit while West still had the ♡A for an outside entry.

At the first table. East's ♠4 showed an odd number of spades, which could only be three. West was right to continue spades.

DEAL 114. THIRD HAND VERSUS SLAM

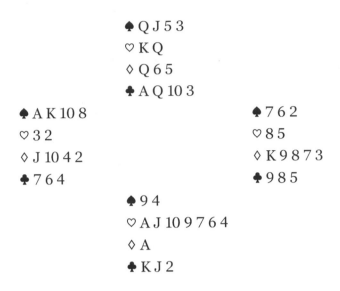

♠ Q J 5 3
♡ K Q
◇ Q 6 5
♣ A Q 10 3

♠ A K 10 8   ♠ 7 6 2
♡ 3 2   ♡ 8 5
◇ J 10 4 2   ◇ K 9 8 7 3
♣ 7 6 4   ♣ 9 8 5

♠ 9 4
♡ A J 10 9 7 6 4
◇ A
♣ K J 2

Not everyone plays the fancy "Namyats" convention, but it is popular in local circles. A Namyats 4♣ showing "a strong four-heart preempt," a 4◇ response says "You play it, partner," and a Blackwood 4NT landed South in this wretched 6♡ slam.

Like many other pairs who play "A from AKx..." opening leads, East and West revert to old-fashioned ambiguous king-leads against slams, so West led the ♠K against this one.

Declarer played low from dummy and the ♠9 from his hand, while East played the ♠2. Seeing the ♠Q in dummy and East's discouraging deuce, West switched to the ◇J. Oops. a "no-play" slam slipped through.

What went wrong with the defense?

West thought that East's deuce was discouraging, but how could East know whether a ♠A continuation would beat the slam? That depended on *West's* length in the suit. All East could do was signal her own spade length so West could figure out whether his ♠A would cash.

In the other room, having attended the same lecture on Namyats, North and South arrived at the same bad 6♡, but West interpreted East's ♠2 at Trick 1 correctly. When West continued the ♠A, East wrote "+50" on her scorecard confidently even before declarer followed to Trick 2.

DEAL 115. THIRD HAND LOW TO CLARIFY

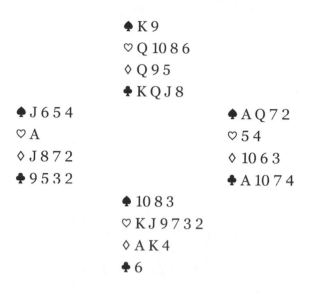

♠ K 9
♥ Q 10 8 6
♦ Q 9 5
♣ K Q J 8

♠ J 6 5 4
♥ A
♦ J 8 7 2
♣ 9 5 3 2

♠ A Q 7 2
♥ 5 4
♦ 10 6 3
♣ A 10 7 4

♠ 10 8 3
♥ K J 9 7 3 2
♦ A K 4
♣ 6

South reached 4♡ on an uncontested auction. With nearly equal holdings in diamonds and spades, West judged (guessed?) to lead the ◊2. A crafty declarer played dummy's ◊9, but East said "No cheap tricks!" as he covered with the ◊10.

South won the ◊A and led the ♡2. In with the ♡A, West had to guess again: was East waiting for another diamond lead with ◊Kx remaining, or did he have the ♠A and ♠Q and need a spade lead through?

West guessed diamonds again, this time leading the ◊J. Declarer won the ◊K and ♡K, led clubs, and set up two club tricks to discard spade losers.

Could West have guessed better at Trick 3?

Yes, if she'd wondered, "Why did declarer play dummy's nine instead of trying the queen?" at Trick 1. Then she might have read South for the ◊K. Alas, few defenders know not to turn their cards too quickly to Trick 1.

However, East could have eased West's burden by wondering the same thing. By following to Trick 1 with the ◊3, he could have drawn the road map that would have steered West right later in the defense. Look for ways to help partner go right!

That's exactly what East did in the other room when the board was played again. Then West found it easy to shift to spades at Trick 3.

A LITTLE OF THIS

AND

A LITTLE OF THAT

DEAL 116. THIRD HAND HIGH?
SPOT CARDS MEAN A LOT

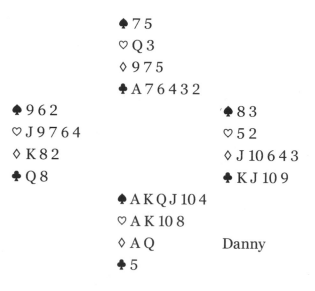

```
              ♠ 7 5
              ♡ Q 3
              ◊ 9 7 5
              ♣ A 7 6 4 3 2
♠ 9 6 2                        ♠ 8 3
♡ J 9 7 6 4                    ♡ 5 2
◊ K 8 2                        ◊ J 10 6 4 3
♣ Q 8                          ♣ K J 10 9
              ♠ A K Q J 10 4
              ♡ A K 10 8
              ◊ A Q        Danny
              ♣ 5
```

North "waited" with 2◊ in response to South's strong, artificial and forcing 2♣, then bid a natural positive 3♣ over South's 2♠ rebid. His 3♠ preference over South's 3♡ next spurred South to gamble 6♠.

All other leads looking more dangerous, West led the ♠2. East covered dummy's ♠5 with the ♠8 to keep dummy from winning a cheap trick.

Declarer continued with the ♡Q and ♡A, then ruffed his ♡10 with dummy's ♠8. Spurning any risky finesse, South returned to his hand with the ◊A, finished trumps and settled for 12 tricks. Making six spades.

How did the precarious 6♠ fare in the other room?

There West also led the ♠2, but anticipating declarer's possible need to ruff a heart in dummy, East appreciated the need to preserve a trump high enough to overruff dummy. So he followed with the ♠3. When South underplayed the ♠4, North quipped, "Gee, had I known my five of spades was a winner, I'd have raised to seven."

Danny, Southeast, retorted, "You may have to eat those words."

North insisted on the last word, saying, "Okay, but hold the mayo."

South tried the ♡Q, ♡A and a heart ruff in dummy, but East overruffed with his ♠8. When the diamond finesse failed, so did the slam.

Little cards mean a lot. Especially the eight of trumps.

DEAL 117. THIRD HAND HIGH OR NOT?

```
                    ♠ J 9 3
                    ♡ Q J 10 3
                    ◇ A K 8 4
                    ♣ Q 8
    ♠ 10 2                          ♠ A 7 6 5
    ♡ K 9 2                         ♡ 6 5
    ◇ J 9 7 3                       ◇ Q 10 6 5
    ♣ A 10 7 5                      ♣ 6 4 2
                    ♠ K Q 8 4
                    ♡ A 8 7 4
                    ◇ 2
                    ♣ K J 9 3
```

When South rebid 1♡ over North's 1◇ response, North raised to 4♡ directly. West led the ♠10, the unbid suit.

East won the ♠A and returned the ♠7 hoping the West could ruff. When West followed, declarer won in dummy and took a trump finesse. It lost, but West could not put East in to lead a third spade that he could ruff.

Losing only the black aces and the king of trump, South made 4♡.

Could 4♡ have been beaten? In the other room, it was.

Before playing to Trick 1, East asked himself if West's ♠10 opening lead could be a singleton. Yes, he realized, but only if South had ♠KQ842.

Whoa! With that spade suit, any sane South would open 1♠. So reading West for a doubleton, East encouraged with the ♠7.

Upon winning the ♡K, West returned the ♠2 to East's ♠A. He ruffed the third spade and cashed the ♣A to beat 4♡.

152

DEAL 118. THIRD HAND: WIN OR DUCK?

                            ♠ K 8 5
                            ♡ 8 6
                            ◇ 9 6 4
                            ♣ A 10 7 6 2
        ♠ 9 6   ♠ A 4 2
        ♡ K Q 10 9 7   ♡ 3 2
        ◇ 10 8 2   ◇ J 7 5 3
        ♣ K Q 5   ♣ 9 8 4 3
                            ♠ Q J 10 7 3
                            ♡ A J 5 4
                            ◇ A K Q
                            ♣ J

After receiving a simple raise, South tried to find a superior game in a possible 5-4 heart fit before bidding game in spades.

Loaded for bear in declarer's second suit, West led the ♠6 to cut down on dummy's ruffing power.

East cooperated by winning the ♠A and returning the ♠2. Declarer won in dummy and ducked a heart to West. West's ♣K shift dislodged dummy's ♣A but now South played the ♡A and a low heart to ruff in dummy.

When East couldn't overruff, South came to his hand in diamonds to draw the last trump. He finished with four spade tricks, three diamond tricks, the ace of hearts and clubs, and one precious heart ruff.

A good start, but a bad finish for the defenders. Do you see how they could have beaten 4♡?

In the other room, East realized that the defenders needed to draw three rounds of trumps, not just two. As he had no other cntry, he ducked the first spade to preserve his ♠A as an entry to lead a third spade.

When West got in with a heart, he continued spades, and only then did East play the ♠A and another trump to kill dummy's ruff and beat 4♡.

DEAL 119. LOWER OF TOUCHING HONORS

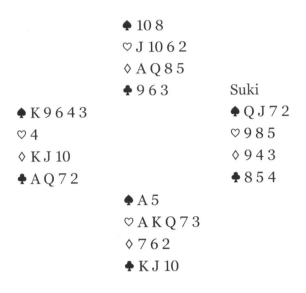

        ♠ 10 8
        ♡ J 10 6 2
        ◊ A Q 8 5
        ♣ 9 6 3   Suki
♠ K 9 6 4 3   ♠ Q J 7 2
♡ 4   ♡ 9 8 5
◊ K J 10   ◊ 9 4 3
♣ A Q 7 2   ♣ 8 5 4
        ♠ A 5
        ♡ A K Q 7 3
        ◊ 7 6 2
        ♣ K J 10

A central precept of third-hand play is *lowest of touching cards*, or more precisely, *lowest card that will do the job*. Partner can draw amazing inferences therefrom. You can never tell when something will matter in bridge. Here's an example of a tiny slip that made a huge difference.

After opening 1♡ and receiving a 2♡ raise, South might have contented himself with a mere game try. East's weak jump raise of West's 1♠ overcall pushed South to bid 4♡ when he might otherwise have tried for game.

West led the ♠4. East, the feminist bridge teacher, believed in giving all jobs that might otherwise be done by male kings or jacks to any available female. Accordingly, she played the ♠Q.

South won the ♠A and then drew the trumps. Then he finessed the ◊Q successfully, cashed dummy's ◊A, and threw West in with a third diamond. Placing declarer with exactly ♠AJ doubleton, West cashed the ♠K. When it held, West had either to lead a third spade, giving declarer a ruff-and-sluff, or break clubs. Either way, West's gander was cooked.

Who fried him?

East, for her play to Trick 1. By playing the higher of equals in an attempt to win the trick, she denied the lower. Had she played a normal ♠J, West could have put her in with the ♠Q to lead a club through.

Any spade honor could do the job of driving out declarer's ♠A, but only the lady could do the job of winning a second-round trick in spades.

DEAL 120. ANOTHER THIRD HAND "HIGH"

```
                    ♠ A K 10 5
                    ♡ 8 6
                    ◇ 10 6 4 3
        Jim         ♣ J 9 3
        ♠ 7 4 2                 ♠ J 9 6
        ♡ K 9 7 5 3             ♡ Q J 4
        ◇ 9 8 7                 ◇ K J 5 2
        ♣ K 6                   ♣ 7 4 2
                    ♠ Q 8 3
                    ♡ A 10 2
                    ◇ A Q
                    ♣ A Q 10 8 5
```

After responding 1♠ to a 1♣ opening, North raised South's jump-2NT rebid to 3NT.
Jim led the ♡5, and South captured Jim's student's ♡Q with the ♡A. Declarer crossed
to dummy in spades, and let the ♣9 ride to Jim's ♣K. To Jim, catching declarer with a
blank ♡J remaining appeared the only hope, so he cashed the ♡K.

Jim's ♡3 continuation went to East's ♡J, but the suit was blocked and declarer took
the rest, making an overtrick. East might have unblocked the ♡J under Jim's ♡K, a
good play that would work if Jim had the ♡10 instead of the ♡9, but on the actual deal
would merely give South a second overtrick.

East said "Jimmy, why didn't you play a low heart to me first? I played third hand
high as you taught me."

Alas, Jim's student had heeded only the word "high" and ignored the rest of the
phrase, "high enough *to do the job.*"

Danny, who speaks in sentences when others use phrases and paragraphs when
others use sentences, says, "Play the *lowest* card that is *high enough* to do the job."

In the other room, West also led the ♡5 against 3NT. East's ♡J lost to declarer's
♡A and West knew to lead low to East's ♡Q upon winning the ♣K. Down one quickly.

DEAL 121. WHEN YOU MUST WORK AT TWO JOBS

```
                    ♠ K 8 5 4
                    ♡ 10 5 3
                    ◊ K Q
                    ♣ K Q 9 2
        ♠ 10 6                      ♠ J 9
        ♡ J 7 6 2                   ♡ A K 4
        ◊ A 8 5                     ◊ 9 6 3 2
        ♣ 8 5 4 3                   ♣ J 10 7 6
                    ♠ A Q 7 3 2
                    ♡ Q 9 8
                    ◊ J 10 7 4
                    ♣ A
```

South opened 1♠ and reached 4♠ via a Jacoby Forcing Raise and a shortness-showing 3♣ rebid. West led the ♡2.

East won the ♡K, cashed the ♡A and continued the ♡4 in hope that West had led from the ♡Q. Little chance! South won the ♡Q, drew trumps, and surrendered a trick to West's ◊A.

Nothing to the play, right? Then how did declarer fail in 4♠ after the same auction in the other room?

There West led the ♡2 also. Except for which minor-suit ace West might hold, and whether his lead was from three hearts or four, ♡Q or ♡J, East had a pretty good picture of the hands. He recognized his *second* job: To give declarer a problem in the heart suit,

East won the ♡A and returned the ♡4. Had South guessed right, East's failure to cash both top hearts would have cost an overtrick, but this was meaningless at IMPs.

Do you blame South for playing low? He lost three hearts and one diamond. Down one.

Defensive falsecards often backfire, fooling partner. On this deal, there was no danger for East in doing so, as it was only declarer who could have a problem. The only danger to the defenders was surrendering an overtrick *IMP*. At matchpoints, by contrast, the risk would be substantial.

DEAL 122. THIRD HAND: SPOT CARDS MEAN A LOT

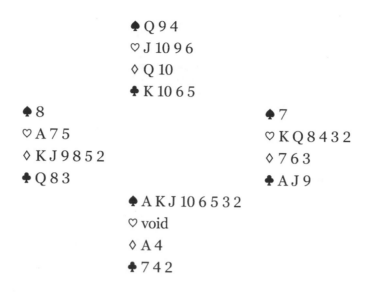

```
              ♠ Q 9 4
              ♡ J 10 9 6
              ◊ Q 10
              ♣ K 10 6 5
♠ 8                           ♠ 7
♡ A 7 5                       ♡ K Q 8 4 3 2
◊ K J 9 8 5 2                 ◊ 7 6 3
♣ Q 8 3                       ♣ A J 9
              ♠ A K J 10 6 5 3 2
              ♡ void
              ◊ A 4
              ♣ 7 4 2
```

Vul against not, East opened a Weak 2♡ Bid in second seat. South bid 4♠. West contemplated sacrificing in 5♡, but thought better of it on adverse vulnerability. He could not be confident that either 4♠ or 5♡ would make.

Did you ever think about suit-quality standards for Weak Two-Bids? Danny achieved some spectacular defensive successes underleading

ace-third in his partners' Weak Two-Bid suits. That's a good suit-quality criterion. Would you be happy if partner underled ace-third in your suit?

West led the ♡5. Declarer played dummy's ♡6, East played his ♡Q. South ruffed with her ♠K. She overtook her ♠J with dummy's ♠Q and led the ♡J from dummy, discarding a club when East followed low.

West won the ♡A and shifted to the ♣3, which was ducked to East's ♣9. When East switched to the ◊7, South rose with the ◊A, led the ♠3 to dummy's ♠4, and took a ruffing finesse against East's ♡K. Ten tricks: Eight spades, the ◊A, and eventually dummy's ♡9 to which dummy's ♠9 provided a late entry.

In the Closed Room, 4♠ failed. Who erred in the Open Room?

East at Trick 1 when he threw his lady to the wolves. The opening lead marked South with ♡A7 or a void. The ♡8 would have sufficed to force South to win the ♡A or ruff. Then the loser-on-loser play would fail.

DEAL 123. THIRD HAND HIGH BUT NOT TOO HIGH

                         ♠ K 7 3
                         ♡ A J 3
                         ◇ Q 9 8 7 3
                         ♣ 9 3
        ♠ J 8 2   ♠ Q 10 6 5
        ♡ Q 8 6 4   ♡ K 10 5
        ◇ J 5 4   ◇ 6
        ♣ A J 8   ♣ K 10 6 4 2
                         ♠ A 9 4
                         ♡ 9 7 2
                         ◇ A K 10 2
                         ♣ Q 7 5

After a limit raise, South rested in 3◇. West led the ♡4, declarer played the ♡3 from dummy and East won the ♡K. East's club shift scored two club tricks for the defenders. South ruffed the third club, drew trumps ending in hand, and finessed the ♡J successfully.

Losing two club tricks and one trick in each major to make 3◇.

Did anybody do anything wrong?

Three diamonds was too high. This deal made Danny, who already has an undeserved reputation for conservatism, wonder: should the range for simple raises of minor-suit openings be extended to 11 support points?

Although normal defense beats 3◇, neither North nor South did anything wrong. It was East who erred by playing his ♡K on air.

In the other room, East, reading West's lead as from the ♡Q, realized the need to save his ♡K to beat dummy's ♡J. He won Trick 1 with the ♡10.
No way for declarer to avoid down one after that.

DEAL 124. NOT TOO HIGH TO AVOID THE ENDPLAY

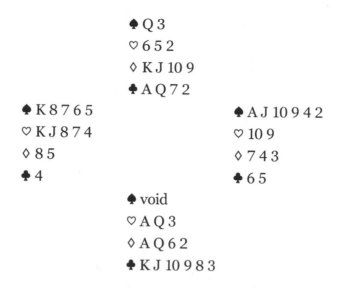

♠ Q 3
♡ 6 5 2
◇ K J 10 9
♣ A Q 7 2

♠ K 8 7 6 5
♡ K J 8 7 4
◇ 8 5
♣ 4

♠ A J 10 9 4 2
♡ 10 9
◇ 7 4 3
♣ 6 5

♠ void
♡ A Q 3
◇ A Q 6 2
♣ K J 10 9 8 3

East's "favorable vulnerability" Weak 2♠ Bid and West's "premature save" 5♠ over South's 3♣ overcall catapulted North-South into the iffy 6♣.

West led a fourth-highest ♠6, declarer played low from dummy, and East played the ♠A. South ruffed, drew trumps and cashed the diamonds, ending in dummy.

When East couldn't cover dummy's ♠Q, declarer discarded his low heart. West won the ♠K but then had a Hobson's choice: ruff-and-sluff, or lead up to South's hearts.

South showed his hand and West folded his cards. Making six clubs.

Could the defenders have avoided the endplay?

Yes. East was to blame. The Rule of Eleven, or common bridge sense, would tell him to play the ♠9, retaining the ♠A to cover dummy's ♠Q later, thus preventing West from being endplayed.

DEAL 125. PLEASE DON'T THROW ME UNDER THE BUS

```
                            ♠ Q J 7 3
                            ♡ K 10 7
                            ◇ K 4
        Rose                ♣ A 6 5 4        Hymie
        ♠ K 5                                ♠ 9 6
        ♡ Q 9 4 2                            ♡ J 8 6
        ◇ A 10 8                             ◇ J 9 6 5 3 2
        ♣ Q 10 7 2                           ♣ J 8
                            ♠ A 10 8 4 2.
                            ♡ A 5 3
                            ◇ Q 7
                            ♣ K 9 3
```

South reached 4♠ easily after responding 1♠ to North's 1♣ opening.

Rose was playing with Hymie, and led the ♡2. Declarer played low from dummy and captured Hymie's ♡J with his ♡A.

Declarer had no way to avoid losing one trick each in spades, diamonds and clubs, but he was able to take a heart finesse to avoid losing a heart. Making 4♠.

Rose looked at Hymie tearfully and asked, "Did you think we had a flat tire, dear?" What did she mean by that?

Hymie had thrown a jack under the bus. He should have relied on Rose to have underled the ♡Q, not the ♡A, and hoped she had the *nine*. That was his only chance to set up a trick in hearts.

When South declared 4♠ in the other room, West also led the ♡2. Realizing the futility of throwing the ♡J under declarer's ♡A, East covered dummy's ♡7 gently with the ♡8. South won the ♡A. West got in with his tricks in the other suits and was able first to dislodge dummy's ♡K and then to cash the ♡Q for the setting trick.

DEAL 126. WAKE UP LITTLE SUSIE

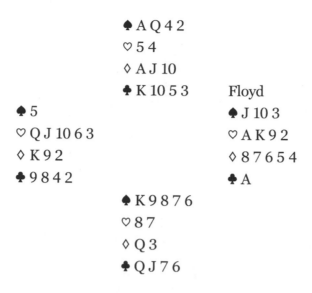

```
                         ♠ A Q 4 2
                         ♡ 5 4
                         ◊ A J 10
                         ♣ K 10 5 3      Floyd
       ♠ 5                               ♠ J 10 3
       ♡ Q J 10 6 3                      ♡ A K 9 2
       ◊ K 9 2                           ◊ 8 7 6 5 4
       ♣ 9 8 4 2                         ♣ A
                         ♠ K 9 8 7 6
                         ♡ 8 7
                         ◊ Q 3
                         ♣ Q J 7 6
```

Floyd, East, dealt and opened 1◊ and received a 1♡ response from West. When North doubled for takeout, Floyd raised to 2♡. South bid 2♠ and was eventually pushed to 4♠ in an auction where nobody knew who was saving against whom.

West led the ♡Q. One yawn later, Floyd encouraged with the ♡9. West duly continued with the ♡10, the bottom of her sequence, and Floyd let it hold. Then West led the ♣9 through dummy's ♣K. Floyd won the ♣A, but that was all for the defense, as declarer drew trumps and finessed diamonds successfully.

Could East and West have done better?

In the other room, Moshe was East and opened 1♡. South made a skinny 1♠ overcall. West, Little Susie, raised preemptively to 4♡ and sold out to North's 4♠. Susie also led the ♡Q. Moshe knew what he wanted (besides Susie). He overtook her ♡Q with the ♡A, cashed the ♣A and returned the ♡2.

Susie won the ♡10, looked under the table to see if the ♡K had fallen to the floor, but finally woke up to what was going on. Moshe ruffed her club return for the setting trick. Eventually South drew trumps and finessed diamonds successfully, but 4♠ was down one. Moshe's seemingly strange plays to Tricks 1 and 2 served as an alarm clock.

DEAL 127. THIRD HAND LOW

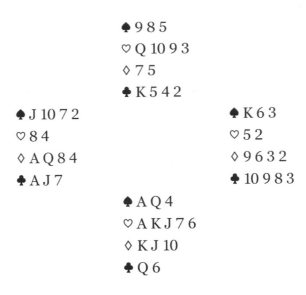

```
                    ♠ 9 8 5
                    ♡ Q 10 9 3
                    ◊ 7 5
                    ♣ K 5 4 2
    ♠ J 10 7 2                    ♠ K 6 3
    ♡ 8 4                         ♡ 5 2
    ◊ A Q 8 4                     ◊ 9 6 3 2
    ♣ A J 7                       ♣ 10 9 8 3
                    ♠ A Q 4
                    ♡ A K J 7 6
                    ◊ K J 10
                    ♣ Q 6
```

West led the ♠J against South's 4♡. Declarer captured East's ♠K with the ♠A, drew two rounds of trumps ending in dummy, and lost a finesse of the ◊J to West's ◊Q.

West could do nothing better than cash the ◊A and lead a third diamond. Declarer discarded dummy's ♠8, drove out the ♣A and claimed his contract.

Why did 4♡ fail in the other room, where Jim sat West? Did Jim do anything special to beat it?

Jim led the ♠J too, but his client had learned to stop and think before playing to Trick 1. The lead marked declarer with the ♠Q, but who did she think had the ♠A? Jim?

East's job was to dislodge South's two spade stoppers, the ♠A and the ♠Q. No need to send a man and a boy to do just one of those jobs when acting separately they could do both. So East merely encouraged with the ♠6.

South won the ♠Q, but when Jim got in with the ◊Q, he was able to continue the ♠2 without blowing a trick. Only then did East put the ♠K to work at the man's job of driving out declarer's ♠A.

Eventually, Jim's ♠10 took the setting trick.

DEAL 128. UGLY DUCKLING OR BEAUTIFUL SWAN?

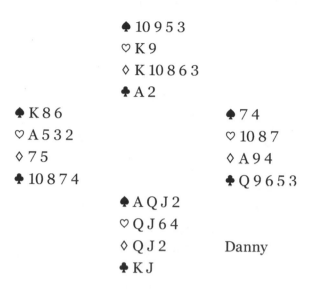

♠ 10 9 5 3
♡ K 9
◊ K 10 8 6 3
♣ A 2

♠ K 8 6
♡ A 5 3 2
◊ 7 5
♣ 10 8 7 4

♠ 7 4
♡ 10 8 7
◊ A 9 4
♣ Q 9 6 5 3

♠ A Q J 2
♡ Q J 6 4
◊ Q J 2   Danny
♣ K J

At both tables, South reached 4♠ via a Stayman auction, and West led the ◊7.

In the Open Room, East won the ◊A and South dropped the ◊J. Declarer hoped he might dissuade East from returning a diamond for West to ruff. East returned a diamond anyhow, but West followed suit and dummy won. Declarer floated dummy's ♠10, losing a finesse to West's ♠K, but the ♡A was the only other trick for the defense. Making 4♠.

Danny, Southeast, turned to South, his kibitzee and said, "Looks like a flat board. Four spades can be beaten, but East has to duck the first diamond to beat it, and he cannot know to do so. He'd look pretty silly if West had led a singleton seven of diamonds and he'd ducked."

In the Closed Room, however, Jim was East and reported that he had ducked the first diamond and beaten 4♠. Danny shook his head. "You shouldn't have. Your partner's lead could have been a singleton."

"No, it couldn't," said Jim. "Our opponents bid hearts before spades with four cards in each when replying to Stayman. South bid two hearts first. Then he bid four spades over North's three notrump, I knew my partner's ◊7 wasn't a singleton or declarer would be 4-4-4-1. Defense is much easier when you pay attention to your opponents' bidding."

DEAL 129. THIRD HAND: ENCOURAGE OR NOT? THEN WHAT?

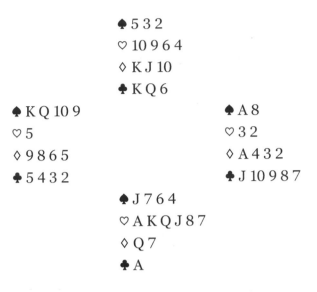

                 ♠ 5 3 2
                 ♡ 10 9 6 4
                 ◊ K J 10
                 ♣ K Q 6

♠ K Q 10 9   ♠ A 8
♡ 5   ♡ 3 2
◊ 9 8 6 5   ◊ A 4 3 2
♣ 5 4 3 2   ♣ J 10 9 8 7

                 ♠ J 7 6 4
                 ♡ A K Q J 8 7
                 ◊ Q 7
                 ♣ A

South reached 4♡ on a uncontested auction. West led the ♠K. East did well to overtake with the ♠A and return the ♠8. West won the ♠9 and continued with the ♠Q.

Good news for East? Not really, for he needed to find a discard. Would the ◊4, the suit to which he wanted West to shift, be high enough?

Would the ♣7, the suit to which he didn't want West to shift, be low enough? He flipped a mental coin and it landed tails. He tried to remember the code, and finally recalled that heads indicated the higher suit and tails indicated the lower, so he discarded the ♣7, the lower suit, playing his lowest to beg for a diamond shift.

However, West shifted to clubs. Curtains! South won, drew trumps ending in dummy, threw diamonds on dummy's ♣KQ, and made 4♡.

Whose fault was it that East's ◊A, the setting trick, went away?

West's for failing to notice that the ♣7 could only be East's lowest, but East's fault also. In the other room, East didn't give West a chance to err. He ruffed West's ♠Q at Trick 3 and cashed the ◊A, the setting trick.

Alternatively, East might have cashed the ◊A before returning West's spade lead at Trick 2.

DEAL 130. QUEEN'S GAMBIT

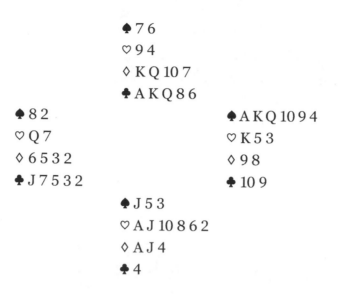

        ♠ 7 6
        ♡ 9 4
        ♢ K Q 10 7
        ♣ A K Q 8 6

♠ 8 2   ♠ A K Q 10 9 4
♡ Q 7   ♡ K 5 3
♢ 6 5 3 2   ♢ 9 8
♣ J 7 5 3 2   ♣ 10 9

        ♠ J 5 3
        ♡ A J 10 8 6 2
        ♢ A J 4
        ♣ 4

Despite East's 1♠ overcall, South reached 4♡. After winning the first two spades with the ♠Q and ♠K, East continued with the ♠A. With nothing worth discarding and having a trump higher than any of dummy's, West in the Open Room ensured a trick for his ♡Q by ruffing with her.

Alas, that was all for the defense. Winning the diamond shift in dummy, declarer floated dummy's ♡9, and when it held, he repeated the trump finesse to pick up East's ♡K and claim the rest.

How did the defenders defeat 4♡ in the Closed Room?

At Trick 3, West discarded instead of ruffing. Declarer ruffed in dummy, but now with only one trump left in dummy had two trump losers.
Down one.

Did West risk losing the ♡Q by declining to ruff with her while he could?

Consider how declarer would have played if his heart holding were ♡AKJ10xx or ♡AKJ10xxx. Would he have played to drop West's doubleton ♡Q, or would he have taken a losing finesse?

DEAL 131. DÉJÀ VU?

Dr J has an angelic bedside manner, but Danny has a bit of the Devil in him. So he insists on presenting the previous deal in his own devilish style, withholding knowledge of partner's hand. Can you stand the repetition?

Bor-ing!

          ♠ 7 6
          ♡ 9 4
          ◊ K Q 10 7
          ♣ A K Q 8 6

♠ 8 2
♡ Q 7
◊ 6 5 3 2
♣ J 7 5 3 2

Despite East's 1♠ overcall, South reaches 4♡. After winning the first two spades with the ♠Q and ♠K, East continues with the ♠10. Declarer covers with the ♠J. What now?

Well, did you learn anything from the previous lesson deal? Or is Danny messing with your mind?

Okay, at Dr J's insistence, Danny will give you some clues, but that's all you get. Instead of the confessions that the criminals in *Midsomer Murders* make to Chief Inspector Tom Barnaby at the end, explaining why they "had to kill" their victims, all you get from Danny are more questions.

(1) Where is the ♣A? Please don't look underneath the table.

(2) East has three hearts: what are they?

(3) Will you mess up like West did in the Open Room on the last deal?

DEAL 132. THIRD HAND LOW TO GIVE PARTNER A SECOND CHANCE

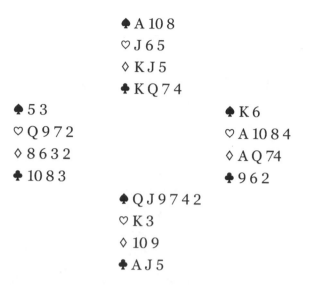

```
                    ♠ A 10 8
                    ♡ J 6 5
                    ◇ K J 5
                    ♣ K Q 7 4
   ♠ 5 3                          ♠ K 6
   ♡ Q 9 7 2                      ♡ A 10 8 4
   ◇ 8 6 3 2                      ◇ A Q 7 4
   ♣ 10 8 3                       ♣ 9 6 2
                    ♠ Q J 9 7 4 2
                    ♡ K 3
                    ◇ 10 9
                    ♣ A J 5
```

South opened 1♠ as dealer and reached 4♠ on an uncontested auction. West led the ♡2 and declarer played low from dummy.

Bemoaning the fact that he had not been the dealer, in which case he would have opened 1◇ and no doubt received the diamond lead that could probably beat 4♠ easily, East won the ♡A and returned the ♡4.

South won and started trumps. After losing a trump finesse, declarer drew the last trumps and discarded a diamond on dummy's long club. Eventually he lost a diamond, making four spades.

After the opening lead, was there any successful defense?

In the other room, East found a way to beat 4♠. He knew from South's opening bid that South had the ♡K, and from West's lead of the ♡2 that the ♡K had a bodyguard. He played the ♡10 to Trick 1 to create a heart entry to West's hand. Then, upon winning the ♠K, he led the ♡4 to West's ♡Q. This time West knew what to lead: the ◇8. Two diamond tricks: down one!

Do you see how declarer could have thwarted this killing defense?

That's right: by playing second hand high, dummy's ♡J, to Trick 1.

DEAL 133. PUNCH AND COUNTERPUNCH

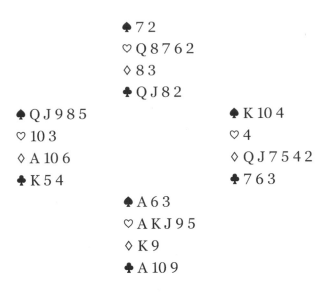

```
              ♠ 7 2
              ♡ Q 8 7 6 2
              ◊ 8 3
              ♣ Q J 8 2
♠ Q J 9 8 5                    ♠ K 10 4
♡ 10 3                         ♡ 4
◊ A 10 6                       ◊ Q J 7 5 4 2
♣ K 5 4                        ♣ 7 6 3
              ♠ A 6 3
              ♡ A K J 9 5
              ◊ K 9
              ♣ A 10 9
```

After a 1♡ opening and a 1♠ overcall, North and East each raised. South's jump to 4♡ ended the bidding. Declarer recognized the danger of a diamond lead coming through her, so she ducked West's ♠Q opening lead.

She won the spade continuation with the ♠A, cashed the ♡A and led the ♡9 to dummy's ♡Q to finish drawing the trumps.

After losing a club finesse to West, she was able to discard a diamond on dummy's fourth club. She lost one spade, one diamond, and one club. Making 4♡.

South did well by keeping the Danger Hand off lead, but the defense slipped. How so?

In the other room, after the same auction and opening lead, East overtook West's ♠Q with the ♠K to try to obtain the lead. Declarer had no winning options.

If he ducked, East would lead a diamond. So South won, cashed the ♡A and led the ♡9 to dummy's ♡Q. South floated dummy's ♣Q, which lost to West's ♣K.

Now it was West's turn to shine. Trusting East to have the ♠10 for her overtaking play at Trick 1, West led the ♠6. East won the ♠10 and shifted to the ◊Q to put the kibosh on the contract.

Special thanks to Michael Lawrence for this theme of punch and counterpunch.

DEAL 134. SACRIFICE THE QUEEN?

```
                    ♠ A K J 5 3
                    ♡ J 10 6
                    ◇ A Q 8 4
                    ♣ 2
    ♠ 8 6                          ♠ Q 10 9 7
    ♡ K 9 7 2                      ♡ Q 8 4 3
    ◇ K 10 5 2                     ◇ 9 6
    ♣ A 10 3                       ♣ 9 5 4
                    ♠ 4 2
                    ♡ A 5
                    ◇ J 7 3
                    ♣ K Q J 8 7 6
```

Playing *invitational single-jump shifts at the three-level*, North-South reached 3NT. West led a fourth-highest ♡2 and declarer played the ♡10 from dummy. The right play for East is the ♡8. Why?

Consider possible holdings from which West would lead the ♡2: (a) ♡ Kxxx and (b) ♡ Axxx.

In (a), declarer has two heart tricks regardless. In (b), declarer has two heart tricks if East throws the ♡Q under his ♡K. But he has only one heart trick if East merely encourages with the ♡8, as declarer's ♡K will fall under West's ♡A on the second round. But not this time.

Here the best play for the suit is not the best play for the deal. East's task here is not to maximize the number of heart tricks but to *kill the entry* to declarer's long clubs. East must sacrifice the ♡Q, and perhaps a heart trick by playing her to Trick 1. After knocking out the ♣A, declarer had nine tricks: two spades, two hearts, one diamond, and five clubs. Making 3 NT.

"Partner, didn't you ever hear of third hand high," asked West.

Who was correct and why?

East's reasoning is *usually* correct. But here it was crucial to dislodge South's entry to his clubs. In the other room, East's ♡Q did so at Trick 1.

Whether declarer won or ducked, he was never going to see those clubs. With his clubs stranded, declarer went down two.

DEAL 135. ANOTHER PLAY FROM MARS

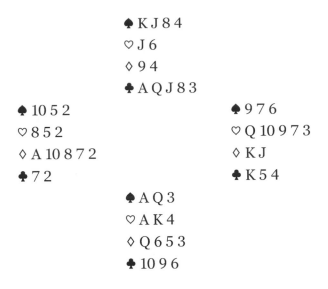

♠ K J 8 4
♥ J 6
♦ 9 4
♣ A Q J 8 3

♠ 10 5 2   ♠ 9 7 6
♥ 8 5 2   ♥ Q 10 9 7 3
♦ A 10 8 7 2   ♦ K J
♣ 7 2   ♣ K 5 4

♠ A Q 3
♥ A K 4
♦ Q 6 5 3
♣ 10 9 6

South opened 1NT and reach 3NT via Stayman. West led the ◊7 to East's ◊K and declarer let East's ◊J return hold Trick 2. Eventually South lost a club finesse but still took ten tricks.

"Flat board," said South. "We'll never get back the 11 IMPs we lost on Board One when they bid that lucky six clubs." Wrong! His teammates returned to compare scores at the end of the match.

"Board Two? Down one in three notrump. Win 12," said East.
"How did you beat it?" asked South. "Looks like a pianola."

"Well, it wasn't," answered East. "I like to make my own kind of music. When Michelle led the seven of diamonds, I knew from the Rule
of 11 that declarer had only one diamond higher.
If that diamond were the ace, then Michelle had the queen of diamonds and at most two high-card points elsewhere, the worthless queen of spades or nothing at all. So I credited Michelle with ace-ten-eight-seven and one or two lower. So I played the diamond jack at Trick 1.

Poor declarer! He dared not duck. What if Michelle's lead had been from ace-king-ten-seven-low and she'd had the king of clubs on side?
So the poor soul won the diamond queen, and when I got in with my king of clubs, Michelle was alert enough to overtake my king of diamonds and run the suit."

DEAL 136. A LITTLE HELP PLEASE, PARTNER

```
                        ♠ A Q 8 6
                        ♡ Q J 10 4
                        ◊ Q J 9
                        ♣ 10 7
        ♠ K 5                               ♠ void
        ♡ K 5                               ♡ A 8 6 3 2
        ◊ K 10 4 2                          ◊ 8 7 5 3
        ♣ A K Q 6 5                         ♣ J 9 8 2
                        ♠ J 10 9 7 4 3 2
                        ♡ 9 7
                        ◊ A 6
                        ♣ 4 3
```

Colonel Whiteflag, West, opened 1♣ thinking to reverse into 2◊ next, and North doubled. East raised feebly to 2♣, and South's 3♠ jump ended the auction. Playing Patriach Opening Leads, West led the ♣K showing the ♣Q and continued with the ♣A. East encouraged with the ♣9 and completed his high-low with the ♣2.

Needing three more tricks to beat the contract, West considered two plans. If East had the ♡A with two or more others, a shift to the ♡K could produce two heart tricks and a ruff or overruff. If East had the ◊A, a shift to the ◊2 could produce two diamond tricks and a ruff if East's ◊A were doubleton.

Left to guess, West looked for clues in East's club spots. Noticing East's deuce on the second round, he guessed diamonds.

"Not a good guess," said East after declarer won dummy's ◊J and came to his hand with the ◊A. Declarer finessed spades successfully and claimed nine tricks.

"A little help from you would have been nice, partner," said West.

What help could East have supplied?

A suit-preference ♣8 on the second round would have helped, but East could have spared the ♣J on the second round to be clearer still.

When attitude and holding are known, suit preference applies.

Oh yes, West was watching the spots closely.

DEAL 137. ANOTHER "HIGH" DEUCE

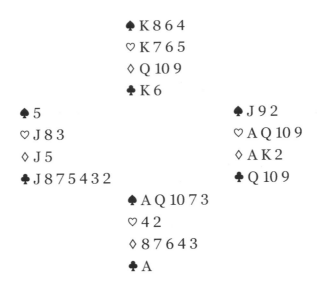

```
                    ♠ K 8 6 4
                    ♡ K 7 6 5
                    ◊ Q 10 9
                    ♣ K 6
        ♠ 5                         ♠ J 9 2
        ♡ J 8 3                     ♡ A Q 10 9
        ◊ J 5                       ◊ A K 2
        ♣ J 8 7 5 4 3 2             ♣ Q 10 9
                    ♠ A Q 10 7 3
                    ♡ 4 2
                    ◊ 8 7 6 4 3
                    ♣ A
```

East opened 1NT. With a choice between showing both spades and diamonds and showing spades alone, South bid 2♠ directly, partly because the spades were much stronger and partly to shut out hearts if West had them. Then he passed North's 3♠ raise.

West led the ◊J and East could smell blood. Reading West for a doubleton, he captured dummy's ◊Q with the ◊K, cashed the ◊A, and returned his last diamond for East to ruff.

Upon ruffing, West starred at that diamond deuce and led the ♣5. South won, drew trumps, and threw a heart on dummy's ♣K to make 3♠.

"Whyntcha give me a ruff with a higher diamond?" asked West.
"Whyncha notice that I didn't have any higher?" answered East.

In the other room, a more thoughtful East anticipated his partner's problem. He won Trick 1 with the ◊A and Trick 2 with the ◊K. Then the ◊2 that he led to Trick 3 didn't look so low.
West noticed East's unusual order of winning the top diamonds. He got the message and led the ♡J to Trick 4. Down one.

DEAL 138. TRUE ATTITUDE, FALSE COUNT

```
                    ♠ 10 7
                    ♡ A 8 6 4 3
                    ◇ A J 2
                    ♣ J 5 3
♠ J 3                                   ♠ Q 9 6 5
♡ 2                                     ♡ Q J 7
◇ Q 9 8 3                               ◇ K 10 5 4
♣ A K 10 8 6 4                          ♣ 7 2
                    ♠ A K 8 4 2
                    ♡ K 10 9 5
                    ◇ 7 6
                    ♣ Q 9
```

South opened 1♠,West overcalled 2♣, and North made a "negative double", then raised South's 2♡ rebid to 3♡. South carried on to 4♡. Too many Martinis before the game?.

Using *Patriarch Opening Leads*, ace-then-king *denies the queen,*

West led the ♣A and continued with the ♣K. Seeing East's high-low, West led a third club for East to ruff, thus killing dummy's ♣J. East took care to ruff with the ♡J, but instead of overruffing, South discarded a diamond loser. Soon declarer drew trumps in two rounds, cashed three outside winners, and crossruffed the rest. Making 4♡.

How did the defense prevail in the other room, where South had the same number of martinis and had bid four hearts?

Unlike East in the Open Room, East in the Closed Room was not a wooden soldier who thought his mission was to "show count, partner."

Instead, here East, with a natural trump trick, asked himself from where the setting trick might be coming, and realized that it was very likely from diamonds. He needed a prompt diamond shift while his partner was still on lead to make one, so he discouraged clubs by following with his ♣2.

West got the message and made the obvious shift to the ◇3. Declarer tried valiantly to make with the ◇A, two top spades and a spade ruff, but could not avoid the obvious four losers.

DEAL 139. WHAT'S IT ALL ABOUT, ALFIE?

```
                    ♠ A 8 6 4
                    ♡ Q 8 5 3
                    ◊ J 9 3
                    ♣ 6 4
     ♠ K 10 3                      ♠ 9 2
     ♡ A K 9 7 4                   ♡ J 6 2
     ◊ 7 5 2                       ◊ K Q 10 4
     ♣ 5 2                         ♣ A 9 7 3
                    ♠ Q J 7 5
                    ♡ 10
                    ◊ A 8 6
                    ♣ K Q J 10 8
```

After a 1♣ opening, a 1♡ overcall, North's "negative double," and East's raise, both sides pushed a little and South wound up in the dizzying heights of 3♠.

Reading East's ♡2 as suit-preference for clubs, and deaf to the auction, West made the unobvious (to say the least) shift to the ♣5.

East ducked the first club, waiting to take the second, but before continuing clubs, declarer led the ♠Q. West covered with the ♠K in case East had a doubleton ♠J. Declarer took dummy's ♠A, returned to his hand with the ♠J and reverted to clubs. East won, and too late shifted to the ◊K.

South took the ◊A and led another club honor. West ruffed as one of dummy's diamonds disappeared. The defense scored one trick in each suit, West's spade trick coming on a club ruff.

How did the defenders beat 3♠ in the other room?

In the other room where East had also raised hearts, East was desperate for a diamond shift, so he made an unusual play, dropping his ♡J under West's ♡A at Trick 1. Taking the auction into account, West read it as suit preference for diamonds and shifted promptly to the ◊7. Two diamond tricks and one in every other suit beat 3♠.

We wonder about that. Did East really need to shout "Diamonds!"?

Not if defenders listened to the bidding and thought "Tricks!" instead of "Signals!"

DEAL 140. THIRD HAND ENCOURAGE OR HIGH AGAIN ?

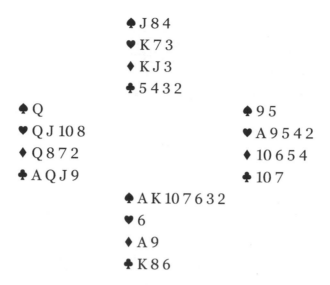

♠ J 8 4
♥ K 7 3
♦ K J 3
♣ 5 4 3 2

♠ Q
♥ Q J 10 8
♦ Q 8 7 2
♣ A Q J 9

♠ 9 5
♥ A 9 5 4 2
♦ 10 6 5 4
♣ 10 7

♠ A K 10 7 6 3 2
♥ 6
♦ A 9
♣ K 8 6

West opened 1♣ and East bid 1♥. South overcalled 1♠. West raised to 2♥ but when North raised to 2♠, South bid 4♠. West led the ♥Q.

Declarer played low and East an encouraging nine. Declarer ruffed the next heart and drew trumps. He took a successful diamond finesse and discarded one club loser on the long diamond. Making four spades, losing one heart, then two clubs later.

Who would you blame for this tragedy?

East. He knew from the bidding declarer had only one heart. West's raise showed four hearts; he would have made a support double with 3-card support. Even though the heart king was in dummy, East needed to overtake with the ace of hearts at Trick 1 to shift to the club ten for three club tricks.

Doesn't it seem every time you play high, you should play low. And when you play low, you should play high? Aren't you sorry you bought this book?

DEAL 141. THIRD HAND HIGH OR NOT TOO HIGH?

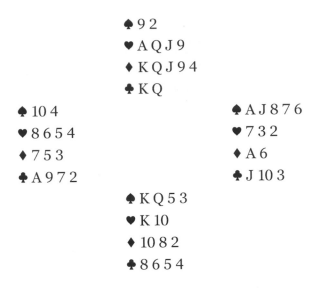

♠ 9 2
♥ A Q J 9
♦ K Q J 9 4
♣ K Q

♠ 10 4   ♠ A J 8 7 6
♥ 8 6 5 4   ♥ 7 3 2
♦ 7 5 3   ♦ A 6
♣ A 9 7 2   ♣ J 10 3

♠ K Q 5 3
♥ K 10
♦ 10 8 2
♣ 8 6 5 4

North opened 1♦ as dealer and East overcalled, somewhat lightly, 1♠. When South bid 1NT, North raised to 3NT. West led the 10♠. Declarer played low from dummy and East considered his options.

Having read this book, he encouraged with the spade eight. What he should have done was count declarer's tricks. Declarer won the spade queen, knocked out the diamond ace and made at least nine tricks.

East wrote me and wanted a refund. I suggested he give a little more thought to the hand before following rules or suggestions.

How should East have been thinking and defending?

At the other table, East realized declarer probably had nine or more tricks if he just encouraged. Two spades, four hearts, four diamonds, and one club. How could ducking by right? East won the spade ace and switched to the ♣ jack.

West won and returned a club. East made another good play by unblocking the ♣ ten (he had also bought my book on unblocking).

When East won the ♦ A, the club return meant five tricks for the defense. Three clubs and two aces.

Well done!

DEAL 142. WHO'S CLUMSIER THAN WHOM?

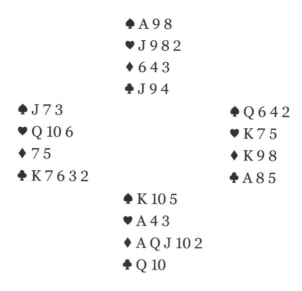

        ♠ A 9 8
        ♥ J 9 8 2
        ♦ 6 4 3
        ♣ J 9 4

♠ J 7 3   ♠ Q 6 4 2
♥ Q 10 6   ♥ K 7 5
♦ 7 5   ♦ K 9 8
♣ K 7 6 3 2   ♣ A 8 5

        ♠ K 10 5
        ♥ A 4 3
        ♦ A Q J 10 2
        ♣ Q 10

Hang around bridge clubs long enough and you'll see amazingly improbable things happen. On this deal, South at each table opened 2NT. South at this table was inept at arithmetic and probably miscounted his points.

Perhaps at the other table, South clumsily pulled the wrong card from his bidding box and didn't notice until too late. It's happened to me.

North's raise to 3NT ended the auction and West led a normal ♣3. Declarer played the ♣4 from dummy and unblocked the ♣Q when East won the ♣A. East returned the ♣8 and West, reading South for ♣Q10 doubleton, ducked South's ♣10.

South overtook with the jack and now had two entries to dummy to finesse diamonds successfully. Then he cashed the ♦A and the ♦K fell. Making 3NT.

How did declarer in the other room go wrong?

By failing to unblock the ♣Q at Trick 1? No, not at all. There, reading West for at most 4 HCP on the bidding, East played the ♣8 to Trick 1. Curtains!

In fact, the final curtain. That's all, folks. Thanks for reading this book. We hope you have enjoyed it and found it helpful. Good luck at the table.

Printed in the United States
by Baker & Taylor Publisher Services